BUSINESS
SMARTS™

ADVERTISING MADE EASY

SUSAN SEWELL

D1005592

PRICE STERN SLOAN
Los Angeles

A TERN ENTERPRISES BOOK

© 1990 by Tern Enterprises, Inc.

Published by Price Stern Sloan, Inc.
360 North La Cienega Boulevard, Los Angeles, California 90048

Printed in the United States of America
9 8 7 6 5 4 3 2 1

Library of Congress Cataloging-in-Publication Data
Sewell, Susan.
    Advertising made easy / by Susan Sewell.
      p. cm. -- (Business smarts)
    Includes bibliographical references (p.).
    ISBN 0-89586-767-2
    1.Advertising--United States. 2.Advertising, American--Case studies. I.Title. II.Series: Business Smarts (Los Angeles, Calif.)
HF5813.U6S45   1990   89-27234
659.1--dc20   CIP

Advertising Made Easy
was prepared and produced by
Tern Enterprises, Inc.
15 West 26th Street
New York, New York 10010

Cover design: Paul Matarazzo
Cover illustration: Donald Richey
Interior design: Lynn Fischer

CONTENTS

INTRODUCTION

I t's been said that the values of a culture are reflected in its advertising, and that is certainly true in America. In the Reagan era, patriotism was in style, and campaigns declaring "Made in the U.S.A." and "Heartbeat of America" proved highly successful. Simultaneously, as mergers of giant conglomerates became widespread, "slice of death" ads, such as AT&T's, which showed workers concerned about picking the wrong telephone system, mirrored employees' fears about job security.

Advertising is also perceived as one of the most exciting, and even sexy, businesses in America. Alfred Hitchcock used it as the profession of Cary Grant's character in the film *North by Northwest.* It is the career of the hip, yuppie characters Michael and Elliott on the hit television show "thirtysomething." And TV's "Bewitched," popular in the 1960s and still being shown on cable, featured an adman—Darrin—as a central figure.

1

But beneath the glamour of production shoots in exotic locations lies a mercurial and gritty business. The business has always been fast-paced, with writers having to churn out ads that will run the next day. But things turned even more hectic in the 1980s, a trend experts expect to continue in the 1990s. Clients, faced with increased competition and tighter advertising budgets, expect more and more of their advertising agencies—sometimes an unreasonable amount, say the agencies. Where once clients and agencies enjoyed trusting, positive relationships that endured for many years, it is getting more and more common for clients to switch agencies, and to do so frequently. The fallout for the agency involved is considerable —jobs are eliminated and agency prestige falls, making it harder to attract new business.

Mergers among the agencies, which have created enormous advertising and ad-based communications companies, have also changed the way the industry operates. Here, too, jobs have been eliminated. More important, clients have begun to worry that they are being serviced by huge conglomerates that care only about dollars and cents and little about the ads they produce. There are virtually no large independent shops left in the country, a state of affairs many regard as unfortunate.

Despite the chaos and changes, advertising remains a fascinating business. It is populated with original thinkers and bona fide characters. As one "creative" who joined a New York agency known for its eccentricity joked, "When they said this agency was just one big family, I had no idea that they meant the Manson family."

Advertising Made Easy has been designed as a short, user-friendly course in the field. Chapter 1, "What Makes a Campaign Memorable?," examines the most celebrated and successful campaigns, as measured by Video Storyboard Tests, a marketing research firm. How do advertisers make the list? How do they stay on it? Some of the most controversial and popular ads of the past are also featured, among them Lyndon B. Johnson's infamous "Daisy" campaign spot, Alka Seltzer's humorous campaign using newlyweds and the innovative "Think Small" print ads for Volkswagen.

Chapter 2, "The Changing Face of Advertising Today: The Agencies," is an inside look at the agencies that spawn the slogans and images that influence millions of Americans every day. These include the legendary Ogilvy & Mather, founded by David Ogilvy, a man who had a very definite idea about what made a good ad—no white type on a black background, for example, because it was "too hard to read." He and Leo Burnett, the man and agency who created the Marlboro Man™, Tony the Tiger™ and a number of America's favorite campaigns, symbolize advertising tradition. The new powers in the trade are the Saatchi brothers, Charles and Maurice, and Martin Sorrell, owner of the WPP Group, who have made their mark not as creative innovators but as financial wizards with dreams of global empires.

If there is a single element that most often separates one agency from another, it is that elusive thing called creativity. The agencies that create the most dazzling campaigns—and do so on a sustained basis—are known as "hot shops." Chapter 3, "The Hot Shops," takes a close look at Chiat/Day, Hal Riney & Partners, Fallon McElligott and others to see what separates them from the hundreds of other agencies in the country.

Chapter 4, "What Is a Client?," examines America's top clients, how a client's advertising department operates and how a client can get the best work out of its agency.

Just how does an advertising agency function? Chapter 5, "How an Ad Agency Operates," goes behind the scenes at a typical advertising agency, examining closely all the duties and responsibilities of the account executive, copywriter, art director, media planner and traffic department. Special attention is paid to the arcane world of media buying, in which agency media planners and buyers must choose from a complex array of advertising vehicles to get the client's message to the right audience.

Chapter 6 covers so-called "Alternative Advertising." With the advent of videocassette recorders, cable television and a host of other competitors to the so-called "big three" TV networks, mass advertising isn't the all-powerful marketing tool it used to be, particularly for advertisers with smaller budgets. By firing more sharply targeted rifles, through the use of such things as direct mail and in-store promotions, ad people are able to reach their audiences more efficiently. Targeted media and special promotions are also the best ways to target growing ethnic audiences such as Hispanics, and other specific segments of the population such as teen-agers.

"Truth in Advertising" is a goal that is not always met. In fact, many people fear what they see as the pernicious influence of deceptive advertising. And, it must be admitted, the popular view of the industry is not flattering. Chapter 7 discusses how government bodies and private consumer groups "police" or monitor advertising to make sure its claims are true.

The best way to understand how the advertising industry operates is to see it in action. *Advertising Made Easy* includes in-depth, chapter-length "case histories" that illustrate three very different, and very important, lessons for all involved in the field:

Burger King,™which had run second to McDonald's™ for years, started to gain some ground on the burger giant in the 1970s by positioning its hamburger as "broiled, not fried." But after that small success, Burger King changed advertising agencies and went through a staff shake-up that saw a veritable revolving door of marketing directors and chief executive officers. Not surprisingly, the company suffered, even to the point of jeopardizing its position as number two in the market.

Pepsi™ was in a similar position—number two behind Coca-Cola.™ But Pepsi chose to stick with its advertising agency, and with an almost-twenty-year-old marketing idea, "The Pepsi Generation." The running cat fight between these two companies is an ongoing fascination for advertisers and marketers alike. The debacle of "New Coke,™" and how Pepsi turned Coke's reformulation into a real marketing and advertising advantage, is just one of the many highlights mentioned here.

Philip Morris is another advertiser that knows the advantage of staying with the same advertising message. Chapter 10,

"Marlboro: Selling the American Cowboy," explores how the company took a failing women's cigarette, Marlboro, and turned it into the world's most popular brand.

Chapter 11 offers answers to a variety of crucial job-related questions: Does a degree help? Should you start out as a secretary and hope to get promoted? How much money can you expect to make?

So you want to be in advertising? Or you've just landed an entry-level job in the field and want to know more? Or you're simply intrigued by the field and want to know how it works? The expert information and real-world advice offered in *Advertising Made Easy* should be exactly what you need to understand a fascinating business and, should you choose to take the plunge, to prosper and thrive in its often thrilling depths.

Chapter 1

WHAT MAKES A CAMPAIGN A CAMPAIGN MEMORABLE?

ood advertising may use emotion, humor, fancy production techniques or some combination of these elements. Whichever the case, the best advertising is usually based on something that creatives call, simply, "The Big Idea."

Which campaigns are America's favorites? Many come from the nation's top advertisers, who have deep pockets when it comes to budgeting for top-notch directors and special effects, and for running the campaigns many times in magazines, newspapers and on television. Occasionally a TV spot that has a small budget makes a big splash because it is a terrific spot, but most of the time the advertising that Americans like best is the advertising that they see the most.

Every year a company called Video Storyboard Tests issues a list of the campaigns that American consumers consider their favorites. In 1984, for example, the top ten consisted of three spots for beer, three for fast food and two for soft drinks. Not surprisingly, all ten were products from companies that have some of America's most hefty advertising budgets.

The top campaign was one that demonstrates the big idea in its purest form. Dancer Fitzgerald Sample's ads for Wendy's™ featured a little woman with a big voice named Clara Peller. As two other women were shown displaying the buns of competing hamburger chains—each sporting a comically small burger to illustrate the point Wendy's was about to make— Clara boomed out, "Where's the beef?" As theater, it was extremely engaging, to say the least. The campaign was also strong strategically: Wendy's had wanted to make the point that its hamburgers filled up the bun, whereas other burger chains were lacking in this regard. Overall, the campaign worked on three fronts: creative, marketing and, most important, sales, which shot up 26 percent during the campaign.

Other campaigns that scored high on the Video Storyboard survey for 1984 were:

- Pepsi, for its campaign using Michael Jackson (created by BBDO)

- Miller Lite,™ which has used the "tastes great, less filling" theme for over a decade (Backer & Spielvogel)

- McDonald's, which used the theme "It's a good time for the great taste of McDonald's" (Leo Burnett)

- Stroh's,™ featuring a beer-drinking dog named Alex (Maschalk)

- Burger King's "Aren't You Hungry?" campaign (J. Walter Thompson)

- Bud Light,™ for its ads showing consumers asking for a Bud Light and getting just about every other kind of light imaginable (Needham Harper Worldwide)

- Coca-Cola, featuring a spoof of the movie *Ghostbusters* and a short-order cook performing amazing feats (McCann-Erickson)

- Kodak,™ showing snapshots of kids learning gymnastics, pets in the yard, etc., all to the theme of "I'm Gonna Get You" (J. Walter Thompson)

- Jell-O,™ featuring entertainer Bill Cosby (Young & Rubicam)

How hard is it to keep a campaign fresh and exciting for consumers? If you are among the top advertisers in the country and can afford to buy the best talent, it's not that hard. Or, at least, that's the conclusion you might come to if you examined Video Storyboard's results just three years later. Five advertisers from the 1984 survey made the list again, but for different campaigns and sometimes for different themes.

The Top Campaigns of 1987

- The number-one campaign in 1987 (and the third most popular for 1986) was produced by Foote, Cone & Belding for the California Raisin Advisory Board using "claymation," a technique in which clay figures are manipulated after each frame is shot to make it appear as if they are moving. In this case, claymation brought to life some hip, cool California raisins, who wore sunglasses and hightop tennis shoes and sang the 1960s hit "I Heard It Through the Grapevine," all for the sake of convincing consumers to eat more raisins. The campaign worked: Both sales and consumer awareness of raisins went way up. Another sign of the campaign's success was that it spawned a number of copycats and a new vogue for the claymation technique itself.

- In second place for 1987 was the Bud Light campaign, created by DDB Needham, using Spuds MacKenzie,™ "the original party animal." Shown in beach clothes or party outfits and always accompanied by three lovely women, Spuds was America's "top dog."

- The number-three spot also won the top award at the Cannes Advertising Festival. Created for Pepsi by BBDO, the commercial played off the company's long-running theme, "Taste of a New Generation." It showed a professor from some future generation at an archeological dig, showing students some relics from the twentieth century, such as a split-level house and an electric guitar. One student, holding up a Coca-Cola bottle, asks the professor what it is. "I have no idea!" the professor exclaims.

• Backer Spielvogel Bates's spots for Miller Lite also featured a long-running theme and captured fourth place. The new tastes-great-less-filling spots featured comedian Joe Piscopo, of "Saturday Night Live" fame, doing a variety of satirical impressions (as a kung-fu fighter, for example).

• McDonald's was voted the fifth favorite for its "New Kid" spot, which showed a senior citizen on his first day of work at McDonald's, and for its "Mac Tonight™" campaign hawking the Big Mac™ hamburger, featuring a model moon crooning new lyrics to the classic song, "Mack the Knife." Both campaigns were created by the Leo Burnett agency.

• In sixth place, in ads created by Hal Riney & Partners, was E&J Gallo's highly successful campaign for Bartles & Jaymes™ wine coolers. The dynamic duo of Frank and Ed, a couple of porch sitters who wax poetic about life and wine coolers, have in fact become extremely popular characters—instant Americana, some say.

• In seventh place was perennial favorite Coca-Cola, with new commercials by McCann Erickson featuring the song "We Are the World" and another spot called "General Assembly," which sought to tie into the summit meeting between President Ronald Reagan and Soviet leader Mikhail Gorbachev. The latter depicted a bunch of kids gathered to sing about peace, and reminded many viewers of Coke's 1971 classic, "I'd Like to Teach the World to Sing," which showed people of all nationalities singing on a hilltop. Coke was also successful with the wise-cracking "Max Headroom™," a character created by applying a mask to a real actor and then enhancing the image with computer graphics. Max caught on quickly with American audiences after making his debut in a British film. His use on behalf of Coke was unusual—cutting-edge technology and media sensations are not the stuff of conventional Coke ads—but it did help Coke appeal to the legions of young cola drinkers.

• In the number-eight spot was a campaign that set American advertising on its ear, mainly because the agency in question (Della Femina, Travisano & Parters, now Della Femina, McNamee WCRS) played to an image that advertising has tried to shake since its inception: All ads lie.

Della Femina turned that perception on its head by employing an actor to project a false smile and fake sincerity and to make exorbitant claims about his product, the Isuzu™ car. While "Joe Isuzu" was "lying," the truth about the car was superimposed in type below him on the screen. For example, in one spot Joe claimed that the car cost only a few pennies; the type below said "not really" and displayed the real price. In another ad, Joe claimed that the car had every feature needed to keep the American family happy, "even a yogurt maker for the kids." Superimposed beneath him was the disclaimer "yogurt maker not included," the agency's way of poking fun at ads saying "batteries not included." Perhaps the funniest spot of the series was one in which Joe fired a bullet, jumped into the Isuzu (first checking his hair in the rearview mirror), then weaved through pylons and jumped out of the car just in time to hold up a target and catch the bullet in his teeth. This unorthodox, even outlandish way to demonstrate the car's speed and handling power worked.

• A campaign for Du Pont's Stainmaster™ carpet came in ninth. This series of spots, done by BBDO, was aimed at demonstrating the product's durability. The ads depicted a small boy with curly red hair—cute or mischievous children are a staple of successful advertising—making havoc for his mom. The boy would, for example, "launch" a plate full of food into the air. The actual launching and scattering of food were shot in slow motion, to heighten the scene's impact. The plate itself was shaped like an airplane, a touch of humor that added to the ad's appeal.

• The number-ten advertiser for 1987 was Domino's™ Pizza, another advertiser that used claymation to good advantage. Domino's was one of the first large chains to focus almost exclusively on home delivery in a market that has become increasingly more and more competitive. To get its point across, the company had agency Group 243 create an animated creature known as the Noid,™ whose mission was to try to ruin Domino's pizzas—by keeping them from being delivered hot, making the cheese stick to the top of the delivery box and other impish deeds.

Rounding out the top twenty-five campaigns were ads for:

- General Foods's Jell-O
- Levi's™ jeans
- Michelob™
- Chevrolet™
- Sprite™
- Long John Silver™ restaurants
- Wendy's
- Seagram's Wine Cooler,™ featuring actor Bruce Willis
- Partnership for a Drug-Free America (hundreds of ads created for free by most of America's top agencies)
- Angel Soft™ bathroom tissue, which showed babies as angels
- Energizer™ batteries, which featured a tough-talking Australian rugby star named Jocko
- Quaker Oats's Kibbles 'n Bits™ dog food
- Oscar Mayer™
- Ralston Purina's Lucky Dog™
- Quaker Oats Tender Chops™

Classic Ads, Now and Then

Ads have always made a deep impression on American audiences. Political advertising, in particular, is usually strong and controversial. One of the first nationally broadcast commercials for a politician serves as a good example. In September 1964, in the midst of the presidential campaign between Democrat Lyndon B. Johnson and Republican Barry Goldwater, the Johnson forces broadcast an ad that came to be known as the "Daisy" spot. It showed a young girl picking the petals off a daisy, interspersed with images of a mushroom cloud from a nuclear-bomb explosion. Only at the end of the commercial were viewers told who had sponsored the spot. The ad aimed to paint Goldwater as a trigger-happy hawk who

> "If an ad campaign is built around a weak idea, or, as is so often the case, no idea at all, I don't give a damn how good the execution is, it's going to fail."
>
> —Morris Hite, in *Adman*

would start a nuclear war, but in fact it backfired: People were so alarmed by the images that the ad was immediately pulled off the air. Apparently, the ad had no lingering effects on Johnson's campaign effort; he won by a landslide.

Popular ads are not necessarily successful ones for the product being advertised. Such was the case with a 1970 ad featuring a new husband eating the first of what, viewers were to understand, were to be many meals prepared by his new bride, who is a terrible cook. At first the husband plays the good sport, eating a huge, mysterious dumpling. But as his wife talks about the other items she has planned for future dinners, such as marshmallow meatballs and poached oysters, the nauseated husband retreats to the bathroom to seek relief with an Alka-Seltzer™ antacid tablet. The product itself was mentioned only in the closing shot, which led many to conclude that the ad actually had a negative effect on sales. In fact, the agency, Doyle Dane Bernbach, may have just been ahead of its time. In the 1980s, several advertisers, such as Nike™ and Levi's, created great awareness for their products by making commercials that barely mentioned the product, and which were more like little movies and stories, as a way of standing out from the barrage of commercial messages.

Because television has such an immediate impact, people tend to remember television campaigns as their favorites much more so than than print ads. But one print ad of the 1960s is known as one of the most famous ever, and is widely considered in advertising circles to be an example of the big idea at its finest. Doyle Dane Bernbach was responsible for what became a widely copied campaign. The ads showed the car, whose odd shape ran contrary to anything Detroit was producing, and a headline reading "Think Small." In an era of gas-guzzling "boats," the Volkswagen ads were notable for their simplicity and for their obvious positioning against big, inefficient car makers. Another ad in the series employed a headline reading, simply, "Lemon," and told how occasionally a defect slipped through during manufacturing, and how Volkswagen took pains to correct the mistake. This, too, was an uncommon approach. It was this sense of surprise, and a clean, simple approach to the ads themselves, which marked the so-called "creative revolution" of the 1960s, sparked by none other than Doyle Dane Bernbach.

An ad that had only a short run during the 1960s but is still shown at industry gatherings and used in advertising courses was part of a campaign for Southern Airways (which disappeared as a result of the airline mergers of the late 1970s). The campaign put the Atlanta-based agency that created it, McDonald & Little, on the map, and was also one of the first efforts of director Joe Sedelmaier, who went on to direct many famous award-winning campaigns, for Federal Express, Wendy's and others. Sedelmaier is well known for taking odd-looking people and exaggerated situations and turning them into comic gold. His style is widely imitated.

The idea for Southern Airways was to show that Southern was the only airline that had no classes, and that without first, second, coach, business or any other class, everyone got the same treatment. To do this, the agency employed an age-old advertising technique: showing how bad the competition is. Thus, a passenger on a competing airline was shown walking through first class, as stewardesses popped champagne corks and confetti flew amid a bevy of happy passengers. Presumably, this passenger, too, was to receive the same treatment. But as he walked toward second class, the stewardess shut the curtain between the classes and the passenger encountered a scene straight out of a prison camp: people in dark, dirty clothing, seated on benches, while a woman in the center of the space stirred a big pot of gruel. A few chickens were running around, just for good measure. The humorous campaign won many awards, but it wasn't just funny: It drove home a very strong marketing point that separated Southern from the competition.

Chiat/Day and its client Apple Computer made several blockbuster spots that were the talk of the industry in the mid-1980s. Apple wanted to position itself as the computer company for entrepreneurs, individualists and anyone who didn't fit into the corporate environment personified by the leader in the computer marketplace, International Business Machines (IBM). One commercial that did the job was notable for several reasons:

- It cost half a million dollars.

- It was directed by leading movie director Ridley Scott (*Blade Runner*) and had a very surreal look.

- It was aired only once.

The entire approach involved quite a risk, but since Apple had built its reputation as a risk-taking company, the association was perfect.

The ad ran during the Super Bowl in January 1984 and was a big hit with the public. In the spot, a huge crowd of men of similar appearance watch a huge screen as a corporate "biggie" preaches. The audience is completely mesmerized; they appear totally brainwashed. Interspersed with the shots of the captive audience is a short-haired woman carrying a big sledgehammer and running as fast as she can. She approaches the screen and hurls the sledgehammer through it, a bold strike against "Big Brother" and for individuality. The end of the spot identifies Apple and tells of the company's new product, which was set to make its debut: the MacIntosh.™

The following year, Chiat/Day wanted to do the same type of "showcase" work, again to run during the Super Bowl. This time, however, problems cropped up. The client and agency argued about whether the spot, which cost well over half a million dollars, should run. But as agency head Jay Chiat explained later, the agency was so convinced that the spot should run that it was willing to pay for its airing on the Super Bowl—a virtually-unheard-of offer in the advertising community. In the end—the argument raged on until the last minute—the client agreed to go ahead, no doubt influenced by Chiat/Day's confidence.

The spot was officially called "1985," but also went by the name of "Lemmings." It showed a long line of pin-striped employees (presumably representing IBM, though they weren't identified as such in the spot) marching in a desolate wasteland, whistling a farcical version of the Seven Dwarfs's song, "Hi Ho, Hi Ho, It's Off to Work We Go." At the end of the spot, it is apparent that the mindless employees are also brainwashed: They are marching, like lemmings, right off the side of a cliff. The ad was critically acclaimed, though it failed to make as big an impact as the previous year's, which was, in any case, a tough act to follow.

Another ad with a very surreal look was one for the perfume Chanel No. 5.™ The spot, which ran in the 1970s, was one of the first to use a movie director, and was also notable for its production techniques and its reluctance to "over-show" the product. Using some funky old music by the Ink Spots, the ads used a number of beautiful images—a man swimming through a pool appearing at a woman's feet, a giant keyboard that plays as a person walks on the keys, and a plane's shadow against an odd-looking skyscraper—to illustrate the campaign's theme: "Share the Fantasy—Chanel No. 5." A different version with the same theme, using French actress Carole Bouquet, was used in the late 1980s.

Other memorable campaigns feature characters who have become so associated with the product that the clients are hesitant to change course because the characters have, in effect, become the brand. Examples include:

- the Jolly Green Giant,™ for Green Giant products

- Josephine the plumber, who pitched for Comet™

- Colonel Sanders,™ the Kentuckian who started Kentucky Fried Chicken

- the Maytag™ repairman, who was lonely because he never had to fix the product

- Madge the Manicurist, who used Palmolive™ dish-washing liquid for soaking her clients' nails ("Madge, I soaked in it!")

Some of these campaigns are so popular that they have been running for more than twenty years. The reason for this is simple, and can be seen in the yearly tabulations of both favorite campaigns and sales: Smart advertisers stick with the tried and true.

Chapter **2**

THE CHANGING FACE OF ADVERTISING TODAY: THE AGENCIES

Corporate mergers and takeovers have changed more than just the names of America's best-known advertising agencies—they've changed the way the entire business operates. Mythmakers such as David Ogilvy and Leo Burnett, whose sophistication and consistency set the tone for much of the industry over the past fifty years, have been supplanted by a new breed of advertising tycoon, exemplified by the Saatchis and Martin Sorrell, whose financial wizardry and global maneuverings have become the new models. A brief look at these personalities and their agencies illustrates what agencies are, how they've changed and what might be in store for the future.

Ogilvy & Mather

"We always lived by the motto that we were 'gentlemen and ladies with brains,'" a former employee of Ogilvy & Mather once recalled. This comment says a lot about the heritage of this major agency, its founder, David Ogilvy, and the high-brow atmosphere that permeated the shop and its employees. Ogilvy, who originally trained as a chef, started his agency in 1948 and quickly became a success. One of his earliest, and still most famous, creations was the Hathaway Man™—the moustachioed gentleman with an eye patch who became synonymous with Hathaway shirts. This tasteful, understated ad was typical of the Ogilvy & Mather approach. Other long-standing Ogilvy clients have included the General Foods company, Hardee's fast-food chain and Kimberly Clark, the paper-goods manufacturer.

Ogilvy himself was an enigma of sorts. In a business in which the general feeling is that rules are meant to be broken, he believed that certain rules should apply when creating ads:

- He felt headlines should make a promise.

- He hated the use of reverse type (white letters on a black background).

- He favored ads with long body copy, so much so that the style became known as the Ogilvy look.

O&M has softened its stance about following its founder's rigid rules about creativity. The agency's spare campaign for American Express is a good example of this new direction. This series of ads uses celebrity portraits (taken by renowned photographer Annie Liebowitz) alongside copy reading "member since 19____."

Ogilvy & Mather made headlines in the 1980s by acquiring majority interest in several of America's top creative shops, such as Scali McCabe Sloves, Fallon McElligott and The Martin Agency. In 1989, O&M itself was taken over by the WPP Group, a British concern that also owns the J. Walter Thompson agency. David Ogilvy, though semi-retired for several years and living in a chateau outside Paris, was greatly distressed by this development. "He [Martin Sorrell, head of WPP] could have at least waited till I died," he said. Ogilvy & Mather was one of the last independent agencies left in America, a vestige, some say, of the industry's earlier glory days.

Leo Burnett

If there is any agency in America that is best known for appealing to traditional, homespun values, it is probably Chicago-based Leo Burnett. The agency does solid work for "blue-chip" clients such as Procter & Gamble, Philip Morris and McDonald's. In a decade of agency mergers and acquisitions, it has made headlines by staying private and sticking to thoughtful ads targeted to middle-class America.

Leo Burnett has also been able to grow by realizing that, in an age in which consumers are blitzed by changing campaigns and slogans, there is a certain comfort level attained by creating recognizable characters who are immediately associated with the product. Leo Burnett created Tony the Tiger and the Marlboro Man, and both are still going strong. In fact, the Marlboro Man is the most successful brand in the world. (This campaign is discussed in more detail in Chapter 10.)

Tradition is very important at Leo Burnett. One sign of the corporate culture is a bowl of apples that sits in the agency's reception area. Burnett, founded in 1935, handed out apples to its visitors during the Depression, and during 1988 gave away half a million pieces of fruit! Corny, perhaps, but a major statement. Burnett himself died many years ago, but his legacy lives on.

Saatchi & Saatchi Advertising

The Britons Charles and Maurice Saatchi, of Saatchi & Saatchi Advertising, are among the new power makers in the advertising world, but they operate at the opposite end of the spectrum from Ogilvy and Burnett. While Ogilvy and Burnett were known for their creative prowess, the Saatchi brothers are known for their financial wheeling and dealing. They have also become feared as acquisitions kings hungry to gobble up agencies in their quest to fulfill their stated goal of becoming the world's largest agency.

Saatchi was the first British agency to make a lot of noise in America on the mergers and acquisitions front, and now owns a number of agencies and consulting firms, including:

- AC&R/DHB & Bess
- Backer Spielvogel Bates
- Cadwell Davis Partners
- Cochrane Chase
- Livingston & Co.
- McCaffrey & McCall
- Rumrill-Hoyt
- William Esty

Saatchi's acquisition of Ted Bates Worldwide in 1986 for $450 million was one of the biggest advertising stories ever. In fact, it may have been a turning point in the megamergers of American advertising agencies—the point at which many observers worried that the British would eventually take over all the great American shops and that the advertising business would soon be reduced to a complex game of financial manipulation.

It is through these subsidiaries that Saatchi & Saatchi can boast major clients such as Procter & Gamble, Johnson & Johnson, General Mills and others.

In 1989, for the first time in memory, agency earnings at Saatchi & Saatchi were down, and the firm announced that it was selling off some of its consulting units. Though its acquisition binge has abated, and though it has slowed its pace of diversification, Saatchi remains a pace-setter in the business.

The WPP Group

Martin Sorrell made news for the same kind of acquisitions as the Saatchis, but with a twist. He led the first-ever hostile buyout of an American agency, the legendary J. Walter

Thompson, America's oldest and one of the last of the independents. His subsequent buyout of Ogilvy & Mather made WPP the world's largest agency holding company, surpassing other agency conglomerates such as Saatchi & Saatchi (which owns McCaffrey & McCall and Backer Spielvogel Bates), Interpublic (which owns McCann-Erickson and Lintas) and Omnicom (which owns BBDO, DDB Needham, and Tracy-Locke).

The forty-four-year-old Sorrell, a former financial director for Saatchi, is an energetic nuts-and-bolts businessman, not given to the flashy excesses that personify other agency heads. Most experts agree that he is the brains behind the dramatic growth of WPP, which at one time was an obscure grocery-cart maker. Besides J. Walter Thompson, WPP also owns:

- Brouillard Communications
- Hill and Knowlton, America's largest public relations agency
- Lord Geller Federico Einstein

Among WPP's clients are Eastman Kodak and Warner Lambert, the pharmaceuticals maker.

How They Stand

Of course, there are many other agencies besides O&M, Leo Burnett, Saatchi & Saatchi and the WPP Group. And there are many others owned by these that we haven't mentioned. The boxes on the following pages give a fuller view of the major players in the advertising industry—who they are and how they rank—as of late 1989.

According to *Adweek* magazine's Agency Directory, the top 10 advertising agencies in the world, in terms of billings, for 1987, were as follows.

Agency	Billings
1. Saatchi & Saatchi DFS Advertising Worldwide	$4,609,437,000
2. Backer Spielvogel Bates Worldwide	$4,068,684,000
3. BBDO International	$3,664,493,000
4. Ogilvy & Mather Worldwide	$3,663,798,000
5. Young & Rubicam	$3,360,000,000
6. McCann-Erickson	$3,300,000,000
7. J. Walter Thompson	$2,988,749,000
8. Lintas: Worldwide	$2,954,000,000
9. DDB Needham	$2,603,101,000
10. D'Arcy Masius Benton & Bowles	$2,553,000,000

Adweek's top 25 was rounded out by, in order:

11. Grey Advertising
12. Leo Burnett Co.
13. Foote, Cone & Belding
14. HDM
15. Bozell, Jacobs, Kenyon & Eckhardt
16. N W Ayer
17. Lowe Marschalk
18. Ketchum Communications
19. Wells, Rich, Greene
20. TBWA
21. Chiat/Day
22. Scali, McCabe, Sloves
23. Campbell-Mithun
24. Wunderman Worldwide
25. Tracy-Locke

(Note: Figures for 1988 and 1989, which would have reflected mergers, acquisitions and other changes in the industry made during that time (such as the purchase by WPP Group of J. Walter Thompson and Ogilvy & Mather), were not available at press time.)

Adweek also ranked the top American agencies for 1987. The top 10 were as follows:

Agency	Billings
1. Young & Rubicam	1,778,500,000
2. Saatchi & Saatchi DFS Advertising	1,679,000,000
3. Leo Burnett Co.	1,550,000,000
4. Grey Advertising	1,500,000,000
5. D'Arcy Masius Benton & Bowles	1,391,000,000
6. J. Walter Thompson	1,388,000,000
7. Foote, Cone & Belding	1,378,700,000
8. Lintas: USA	1,364,000,000
9. DDB Needham	1,178,000,000
10. Ogilvy & Mather	1,169,993,000

The rest of the top 25 were:

11. Bozell, Jacobs, Kenyon & Eckhardt
12. McCann-Erickson
13. Backer Spielvogel Bates Inc.
14. BBDO
15. N W Ayer
16. Wells, Rich, Greene
17. Ketchum Communications
18. Chiat/Day
19. Campbell-Mithun
20. Tracy-Locke
21. Ally & Gargano
22. William Esty
23. Ross Roy
24. AC&R/DHB & Bess
25. McCaffrey & McCall

Though many of the names in the boxes on the preceding pages are listed as individual agencies, they are actually owned by holding companies. The following list illustrates just partially how consolidated the advertising business has become in recent years. In fact, the pace of mergers and acquisitions is so furious that this picture is likely to have changed by the time you read this book.

• WPP Group PLC owns J. Walter Thompson (#6 on *Adweek's* domestic list), Lord Geller Federico Einstein (#37) and others.

• Saatchi & Saatchi owns Backer Spielvogel Bates (#13), Campbell-Mithun (#19), William Esty (#22), AC&R/DHB & Bess (#24), McCaffrey & McCall ((#25), Rumrill-Hoyt (#98) and more.

• The Omnicom Group owns DDB Needham (#9), BBDO (#14), Tracy-Locke (#20), Doremus & Co. (#39), Ingalls, Quinn & Johnson (#51), Rapp & Collins USA (#73) and others.

Chapter **3**

THE HOT SHOPS

I f there is one single element used to differentiate agencies, it is that elusive talent called "creativity." Creativity means many things to many people, but for the average consumer, creativity would be the evocative music that makes him look up at the television screen while reading his paper, the hilarious ad that makes him laugh out loud or the touching campaign that gives him a lump in his throat. The McDonald's Corporation even had a name for that second when the consumer got that "lump-in-the-throat" feeling: the "magic moment."

It is that same magic moment that companies want from their advertising, and the desire to find it often means that big companies will move multimillion-dollar ad accounts from one agency to another in quest of that elusive high. Often the magic moments are found not with the large, established agencies but with a number of smaller, more adventurous "hot shops." It's safe to assume that some of the most memorable TV, radio and print advertising of the 1990s will emerge from the following hot shops, which made their marks in the late 1980s.

Hal Riney & Partners

Hal Riney launched his own agency by buying out the San Francisco office of Ogilvy & Mather. Hal Riney & Partners quickly posted astronomical growth, racking up an astonishing 65 percent increase in new billings in one year alone (industry experts consider 10 percent respectable).

The single element that most new clients cited when naming Riney as its new agency was the shop's ability to give a classic look to almost any product. One of the agency's most noted campaigns was done for Gallo Wines and featured beautiful scenes of happy weddings and family picnics set to classical music. A campaign for Perrier™ showed the French country-side from which the sparkling water comes. Riney himself was often used as the voice-over for TV commercials, and his soft, deep voice was immediately copied by many "sound-alikes."

But the agency is hardly a one-note song. Perhaps its most famous campaign was the one that made good-old-boys Frank Bartles and Ed Jaymes household names—and Ernest & Julio Gallo's Bartles and Jaymes wine coolers one of the top coolers in a competitive new category.

In 1987 the agency did something that still causes a buzz in the advertising industry: It resigned from the E.&J. Gallo business, worth some $70 million, a huge chunk of the agency's work. Gallo had always had a reputation as being one of the most difficult accounts in America, and it eventually wore the agency down. Riney himself was said to have written more than 150 of the Bartles and Jaymes spots (it is rare for an agency principal to get involved on this level), and rumor had it that the agency had presented up to 60 different campaigns to sell Gallo Brandy.™ The advertising industry was shocked, but the resignation only served to enhance the already legendary status that Riney enjoyed.

Fallon McElligott

In the advertising world, hot shops come and go like burned-out meteors, but one hot shop, Minneapolis-based Fallon McElligott, has managed to continue burning brightly. The creative force behind the agency, Tom McElligott, is credited with creating a style of dramatic headlines and gripping graphics that has been widely copied. In fact, Fallon McElligott is one of several hot shops that have brought recognition to Minneapolis as a "hot" advertising city—sparking an industry-wide realization that some of the best work was being done outside major ad cities like Chicago and New York.

McElligott, with partners Pat Fallon (who handled the agency's business side) and Nancy Rice, began as Fallon McElligott Rice in 1981. In seven short years, billings had zoomed to $140 million, primarily on the strength of the agency's creative skills. Stories about the agency were legendary. In the early years, the owners parked in the lobbies of clients who refused to see them, waiting for hours to show the work that they knew would persuade the reluctant clients to sign up the agency. Another strategy the agency used as a public-relations tool to make its name well known as a hot shop was to work on public-service accounts for free, then enter the work in awards shows. Generally speaking, because public-service work is done for free, the "client," such as the United Way or an anti-drug campaign, is reluctant to make any changes in the creative, so public service ads (known as PSA's) are considered great creative showcases. They certainly proved so for FMR. One of the early Fallon McElligott public-service ads, for the Episcopal Church, showed the emblem of a Mercedes-Benz and the headline "Some people worship a more important symbol"; a cross appeared at the bottom of the ad. Recognition came quickly, as did billings. To this day the agency still regularly stomps the competition in prestigious competitions such as the One Show.

Still, the agency has suffered some losses. Nancy Rice left to start her own agency with her husband. Tom McElligott left the shop after creative differences with his partners. But the agency seems to be going strong. Among its leading clients is Federal Express.

Although the Southeast is not usually known for setting trends in the advertising business, two agencies there have captured quite a bit of attention on the creative front. Both are located outside what are considered the South's main advertising centers—Atlanta, Dallas and Miami—proving that great creative has no address.

McKinney & Silver

Based in Raleigh, North Carolina, McKinney & Silver made news by winning the prestigious Steven F. Kelly award for magazine advertising, the only advertising award that carries a cash prize—a whopping $100,000. The winning campaign was its long-running work for the tourist bureau of the state of North Carolina. The ads featured the handmade quilts and quiet water ferries that personify the state's relaxed way of life and were a marked departure from the typical approach used in state tourism advertisements—beautiful shots of landmarks, beaches and the like.

McKinney was also the long-time agency for Piedmont Airlines, although it lost the account in 1988 after the airline was bought out. The agency's work for Piedmont was considered by many to be the best in the industry, again because it ran against convention. To promote a variety of special fares, for example, McKinney and Piedmont used veteran actor McLean Stevenson to show the various prices by comparing the fares to different types of furniture—a recliner for a trip to Texas, for example. The ads proved an effective way of cutting through the clutter, drawing greater awareness to this small regional airline.

McKinney used that same offbeat approach to advertise Norwegian Caribbean Lines. Instead of going with the expected approach—photographs of ports of call, for example—the agency instead showed a child's boat floating in a bathtub and used copy reminding consumers how they had dreamed of taking a cruise ever since they were children.

The Martin Agency

The Martin Agency has less of a recognizable "look" than McKinney, but has made a name for itself by doing great creative work on accounts that are considered some of the hardest with which to do fun, fresh work—agricultural and business-to-business accounts (*e.g.,* sales of copiers or phone systems to companies).

For one television campaign, for a herbicide that kills certain kinds of weeds, the agency built a replica of the weed that could move like a human. The spots showed farmers listening to the radio, watching TV or talking on the phone to other farmers about how the herbicide killed weeds. As the discussion goes on, the "human" weed snakes up a telephone pole to pull down the wires, sneaks in a window to pull the television plug, enters a barn to knock the radio over—generally raising havoc on all fronts. The spot was extremely funny, and increased awareness of the product with its target audience.

The agency also took on a project for the nonprofit group People for the Ethical Treatment of Animals that proved so effective that many people found themselves unable to look at the ads. Actual pictures of experiments performed on animals were shown—for instance, a hammer being used to crush a monkey's skull; an electrode being implanted in a live rabbit; a monkey hooked up to what looks like a primitive electric chair. One of the headlines commented on doing "experimental work on your body—with you still in it." The ads were horrifying, but very effective in driving home the conditions that laboratory animals face.

The creatives at the Martin Agency tend to be so driven by their work that many continue doing it in their off-agency hours. In fact, several creatives in the agency started what later became an industry trend by forming an after-hours agency called Drinking Buddies Inc. They commonly gathered at a local bar, and drew their ideas for ads on cocktail napkins. Since Drinking Buddies did work for nonprofit agencies only, and only took money for the cost of materials and production, there was no conflict with agency work.

Chiat/Day

Chiat/Day is hardly an overnight success story. Indeed, the long hours logged by agency employees prompted one to print up T-shirts reading "Chiat Day and Night."

The agency made major headlines in the 1980s with its offbeat sense of humor and California style. Based in Los Angeles, the shop was responsible for many of the campaigns that caused Americans to smile. One of the most enjoyable was the California Cooler™ spots featuring vintage beach scenes and old classic songs like "Louie Louie." The agency also received many kudos for its spare ads for Nike, which featured famous athletes doing their thing with the Nike theme superimposed at the bottom. The spare copy made many observers say those ads bordered on art. Other successes have included Levi's 501™ jeans, with its street scenes, and Nike ads featuring Randy Newman's popular song "I Love L.A."

Agency head Jay Chiat has become something of a spokesperson for hot shops and others who do the unconventional in the advertising business. One of his most oft-repeated quotes sums up the joy and difficulties faced by these small, yet growing creative ad houses: "I want to see how big we can get before we get bad."

Chapter 4

WHAT IS A CLIENT?

Very simply put, a client is the individual or company that wishes to advertise. It can be a giant corporation looking to create a nationwide, multimedia (print, radio and television) campaign for an entire line of goods, or the corner drugstore that needs a newspaper ad to publicize its weekly specials.

Most commonly, clients call on advertising agencies to help them prepare and place the advertising. Some large companies, in a desire to save money and exert control over the process, possess what is known as an "in-house agency," that is, its own advertising staff that functions just like an independent advertising agency. The main idea behind having an in-house agency is that the company that wishes to advertise does not have to pay the commission that most advertising agencies charge as their fee. This commission is generally 15 percent of the client's total advertising budget.

Not surprisingly, the nation's largest companies in terms of sales are also the nation's top advertisers.

In 1988, the top 10 advertisers were:

- Philip Morris
- Procter & Gamble
- General Motors
- Sears Roebuck
- Ford Motor Co.

- PepsiCo
- McDonald's Corp.
- AT&T
- RJR Nabisco
- Ralston Purina

Although the titles and responsibilities vary from company to company, most corporations that use advertising will have a department headed by a **director of advertising** or **director of marketing**. If the department is quite large, there will often be several associates, each with a title such as **assistant director of advertising**. At the largest companies, the responsibilities for marketing and advertising are handled by a **brand manager**, who makes the decisions about a specific product, *e.g.*, Sprite soft drinks or Quaker Oats cereal.

The client determines how much money is to be committed to advertising, what the message should be and the selection of the advertising agency to prepare that message.

After a budget is determined, many companies launch an "agency search"—that is, a review of a number of agencies to select which one will get the job. The review can include as few or as many agencies as the client desires. Often a client will talk only to agencies that bill more than a certain amount of money per year, or to those who have had previous experience with a similar type of product. Other criteria include an agency's geographic location, the desire to work with well-known creative talent and the fact that some agencies are more proficient at either print or television and radio advertising.

One consideration that can prevent some agencies from being included in a review is a conflict of interest, meaning simply that the agency already handles a similar product that is a competitor to the client launching the review. In some cases, if the prospective client's budget is larger or the product more enticing, the agency may decide to resign its current client to pursue the new business. The trade papers and marketing/advertising columns of newspapers are filled with news of agency reviews—such news is of public knowledge in the industry and agencies can decide to try for the job even if not invited—and conflicts are often part of the equation.

> "In new business, there is one strategem which seems to work in almost every case: Get the prospect to do most of the talking. The more you listen, the wiser he thinks you are."
> —David Ogilvy, in *Confessions of an Advertising Man*

The length of the review is determined by the client. There have been many celebrated reviews that lasted for more than a year. Why so long? Sometimes, as with government accounts that are mandated by law to hold an agency review at set intervals, it's just the bureaucracy involved. Management changes at the companies doing the review can also send everyone back to square one at any time along the way. Sometimes, too, companies start with an incredibly wide "net" of potential advertisers—as many as 100—that is then narrowed first to 70, then to 30, and so on. Most companies, however, start with a more precise notion of how many advertising agencies will be included in the review, and often the specific names of those agencies. These clients are eager to make their decision in a couple of months so that the actual advertising can be put into place.

Often the review process involves narrowing the list of competitors several times, in a sort of beauty contest among the agencies. Besides formal presentations of their capabilities and the people who will actually be working on the account, agencies sometimes create speculative campaigns, known as "spec work," to give the client some idea of what type of advertising they will prepare should they win the account.

Speculative campaigns are something that most agencies dislike, for a number of reasons. Needless to say, working up new ideas, using many hours of valuable staffers' time and actually producing a rough version of the ads can get very expensive. Some clients pay for this spec work, but the vast majority do not. There have been cases in which the bills ran up to half a million dollars for some of the largest advertisers.

Some clients hold reviews periodically just to see "what's out there" in terms of new ideas and new talent. In these cases, the current agency, known as the incumbent, may or may not be included in the review, depending on the client.

When a big piece of new business is at stake, the competition is intense and the pressure that accompanies the reviews is extreme for both the agencies involved and the client. Agencies are worried about many things:

• whether the client will steal the speculative ideas it has created and then stick with its current agency (companies are on the "honor system" when it comes to this)

• how to keep the morale of the presenters up (preparing presentations often requires working around the clock; conversely, the process can drag on for months with no word of a decision)

• how to stand out from the competition

Most large advertising agencies have a standard pitch that uses their ads as a kind of propaganda device to convince the client that they are the right choice. Of course, there are customized pitches as well. One agency even had its president dress up in a gorilla suit in order to win a local zoo account.

The "notice me and I'll win the account" tactic paid off handsomely for two Southeastern agencies. When W.B. Doner, in Baltimore, was pitching the Arby's account, and Bozell & Jacobs, of Atlanta, was pitching Valvoline oil, both used advertising as a way of drawing attention to themselves. The agencies literally "painted the town" with billboard ads strategically placed where the potential clients' executives were sure to see them—for example, on commuter routes into and out of town. Both agencies won the accounts.

> "All clients are the same. They say, 'Can you do something that's completely original but something we've seen before so we're familiar with it?'"

The advertiser/client also worries about the pressures that accompany agency reviews. A mistake can be very costly in lost time and money. In recent years, making the decision about which advertising agency to use has been complicated by the number of agencies that are willing to stray from the standard 15 percent commission, a practice known as "low-balling." Some advertisers may decide to go with the agency offering the cheapest price—making the decision based on finances, even though the main thing an advertising agency is selling is ideas.

Once the decision on an agency is made, the client and agency begin working on a new campaign. The client works with the shop, deciding on positioning against the competition, what media will be used and what the creative message should be.

There are many notorious stories about bad relationships between clients and agencies. One large, prestigious client was supposedly so heartless that it insisted on continuing with an agency presentation even when one of the account executives had an epileptic seizure. This is an exaggerated case, of course, but it illustrates an important point: A client and an agency work so closely together that the result is a relationship that is only slightly different from a marriage. When things go well, everyone is happy; when things go wrong, the relationship takes on the look and feel of a messy divorce case.

How can clients get the best work out of their advertising agencies? Most problems seem to crop up when either the client or the agency is not communicating or being totally honest. Advertising is a very fast-paced business, with a million situations in which mistakes might be made. Creating advertising that works involves several key things:

A close and honest relationship

The best client comes totally clean with the agency about the product, giving its advertiser as much detail as possible about its problems and advantages, as well as information about the competition. Sizing up the product and how it is doing is one of the key phases that an agency goes through to decide how to make it stand out from the competition. (For more about market research, see page 48.)

Chemistry

The most buttoned-down advertisers tend to pick agencies that are very much like themselves. The most entrepreneurial and hip clients also tend to pick agencies that are not afraid to take a chance. (Apple Computer, Nike and the Chiat/Day agency spring quickly to mind.)

Letting the advertising agency do its job

In other words, clients should try not to compete with the advertising agency. Agencies should be given good information, and then left to do their job. Of course, there needs to be frequent communication and interaction between agency and client. Sometimes, though, this gets out of hand. Agencies loathe clients who:

- actually write the copy for the print ad
- offer "great" ideas
- ask that relatives be the talent in the advertising campaign

Avoiding Advertising by Committee

Another big complaint on the part of advertising agencies is that the advertising has to be approved on too many levels. Needless to say, everyone has an opinion, and the advertising slowly gets changed so that it eventually looks nothing like the original—and all too often diluted in its impact. Agencies like dealing with one or two people, when possible.

Some of the smartest agencies, such as Chiat/Day, try to involve the client in the creative process from the very beginning. In the old days it was more common to get the original directive from the client, work hard on a campaign for months and then spring the new campaign on him or her at a presentation after a long space of time in which the client had no involvement. Under the system that Chiat/Day uses, the client is told of each and every step of the creative process, and he or she becomes, with the agency, "the owner of the idea." This avoids having the client seeing a campaign months later and not liking it, sending the agency back to the drawing board.

Not all clients are troublesome, no matter how many horror stories agencies have to tell. Some of the nation's top companies have relationships with their advertising agencies that have endured for decades. The bond between Philip Morris and Leo Burnett is a good example. If both parties view the relationship as a partnership (instead of boss and employee), the best results are usually obtained. Agencies have nothing but good to gain from successful relationships with clients: As their brands prosper and grow, so do the agencies' fortunes, with increased ad budgets and new work for the company's other products.

Chapter 5

HOW AN AD AGENCY OPERATES

An agency's single largest asset is its employees. Or, as Leo Burnett once said, "At an advertising agency, the inventory goes down in the elevator every night."

Employees are important in any business, of course, but because advertising relies so much on strategic thinking and creativity, the best agencies are almost always those where the stars—whether in creative, account management or media—do their stuff. Because they are highly sought after, these stars often command six-figure salaries and the many perks that come with such exalted status. What follows is a look at the division of labor within an advertising agency.

Account Management

An account executive is the primary liaison between the client and the agency. The job itself is difficult to describe because it requires performing so many different tasks. Primarily, an account executive communicates the client's needs to the agency personnel who are to fulfill those needs, and smooths the way for the effective completion of all advertising that the client commissions.

Account executives are responsible for talking to the client in the early stages to determine the client's advertising goals. In the most obvious cases, the idea may be simply to move the product off the shelves. In other instances, the client may have something more encompassing in mind. For example, some advertisers want what is known as corporate or image advertising. This kind of pitch is designed not necessarily to sell a specific product but to reinforce the company's name to consumers or to create a good feeling about the company. Such ads serve as a reminder to consumers that "we're still out there, and we care about your business." Examples of this type of campaign would be Coca-Cola Co.'s "Can't Beat the Feeling" campaign and Chevrolet's "Heartbeat of America" campaign.

Once it is determined what direction the client wants to take with the campaign, the next step is to determine the **target audience**—those people who are most likely to buy the product and, therefore, those to whom any sales message should be addressed. For a laundry detergent, that might be women who are homemakers; for a beer product, that would likely be young men.

Another consideration is the choice of media: How can the client and agency best reach the prime audience, in the most effective way? This may mean using narrowly targeted magazines, *e.g., Cat Fancy* or *Chocolate Lovers,* or, if the audience is large and the budget adequate, using TV and/or radio advertising.

Armed with this knowledge, the account executive may now approach the creative department of the agency so that it can begin creating the ads. In ideal situations, the account executive gives the creative department as much information as possible about:

- the client's desires (the message it wants to convey; the goal it wants to achieve)

- the competition (how does it stack up?)

- the target audience (how it feels about the product; what, if anything, it would like to see changed; what it hopes to gain by buying the product)

After the creative department has come up with the ads (we'll be discussing the creative department in the next section), the account executive and creatives present the campaign to the client. (Sometimes there is an interim step in which rough sketches, or "comps," are reviewed before the creatives go too far with any one idea without any feedback from the client.) Although the creatives are usually the ones to make the presentation, the account executive is on the scene to coordinate the efforts and to see that things go smoothly. Traditionally, creatives come up with more than one or two ideas, since clients often disagree with one idea or approach and want to see something else.

Once the client and the agency have agreed on the ads' look and content, the account executive makes sure the ads get produced to the client's specifications. At the same time, he continues to work with the media department selecting the specific media buys for the campaign (the actual media having been decided upon at the outset of the client/agency contacts).

As you can see, an account executive is primarily a facilitator, or, perhaps, a conductor, responsible for coordinating the work of the creative, media and research departments of the agency. As account executives move up the ranks, they sometimes become **account supervisors,** which usually means that they have responsibility for more than one account. In that case an account executive does most of the legwork and the account supervisor makes sure that things are running smoothly and on schedule, and steps in as a trouble-shooter if and when needed.

Creative Department

If there are natural adversaries for the account executive, they are usually the **copywriter** and **art director,** commonly called **creatives,** who make up the backbone of the agency's creative department. This is the part of the agency that is responsible for coming up with the idea or theme of the campaign that the client will run. If account executives by definition tend to be "button-up" and conservative, creatives are just the opposite. Because they are prized for thinking in the abstract, they are generally more offbeat and eccentric than account executives. In most agencies, in fact, it is almost expected that the creatives will be "wild and crazy." (This is not, however, a prerequisite for the job.)

Though creative departments vary from agency to agency, most shops pair a copywriter with an art director to work on one or more accounts. Of course, in the case of a giant client such as a major soft-drink or automotive company, there may easily be a number of creative people assigned to the account, just because of its sheer size.

The copywriter is the person who literally does the writing of an ad, from the headline to the body copy for print, or the script for television and radio. The art director is the person who gives an ad, print, television or radio, its special look—by deciding what kind of type to use, whether to use photographs or illustrations, what moving images and special effects are to be used and how to put these elements together to form an effective whole.

In many cases the first step for the art director/copywriter team is to get together and brainstorm—that is, throw out a number of ideas, the best of which are then given more complete treatment. Often an agency conference room will be littered with hundreds of large sheets of paper, each sporting headline or art ideas—a sure sign that a brainstorming session has taken place. Years ago it was common for the copywriter to come up with the idea or theme for the advertising campaign, but these days ideas can come from either the copywriter or the art director, or both working in collaboration.

The **creative director** is the person who oversees the individual teams of art directors and copywriters. In very large agencies, there may be several creative directors, who report to an executive creative director, whose main job is to oversee all creative work and, often, function as the lead presenter in new business presentations.

> "In the modern world of business, it is useless to be a creative, original thinker unless you can also sell what you create. Management cannot be expected to recognize a good idea unless it is presented to them by a good salesman."
>
> —David Ogilvy, in *Confessions of an Advertising Man*

In the 1980's, some of the most innovative American agencies experimented with a new method fo pairing creative teams. While having one team concentrate on a particular account makes lots of sense, since the team can become very familiar with the brand to be advertised, its customers and its problems, some agencies are finding that it is good to switch teams on accounts to come up with a fresh perspective and new ideas.

It is also not unheard of for agencies to pit creative teams against one another, particularly in new-business presentations, in order to come up with not only the best ideas, but a number of choices from which the client can pick.

The best creative people, and inevitably the ones who are deemed the stars and command the highest salaries, are the ones who are not only talented, but are good salespeople, too. This is a frequently overlooked skill. Creatives must be able to get the account executive excited about the work, and be prepared to defend their work to the client as well. Many stories are told of creatives who have spent hundreds of hours, all their weekends and many overnighters at the office to come up with what they think is the most creative idea, only to have it shot down by the client in the first few minutes of a presentation. Creatives must also understand the product, the client's business and the competition as well as the account exec does, and be able to defend solidly the thinking that has gone into a creative idea.

When the nation's largest advertisers are, in essence, betting millions of dollars that their advertising will work, it is little wonder that they second-guess outlandish ideas from creatives. Indeed, in any given decade there are usually only a handful of clients willing to take chances. The most conservative, which make up the majority, let the gutsiest clients take chances on new ideas or techniques, then follow suit when it becomes apparent that the technique works. Chiat/Day advertising was widely praised for its spartan Nike ads. In a sea of copy-heavy campaigns, these efforts were compared to art and made Nike stand out. It wasn't long before a number of other advertisers jumped on the spare-copy bandwagon.

In the largest agencies—and especially those that do a lot of television commercials—another job falling under the jurisdiction of the creative department is that of **broadcast producer**. The broadcast producer's job is a little like the account executive's: He or she is in charge of every facet of getting the commercial produced, from working with the art director and selecting a production company to keeping the production within creative bounds, on time and within or under budget. The broadcast producer works with the production company in selecting locations for the shoot, gaffers, sound men, makeup artists, food stylists (whose job is to make food look good, even if it has to sit under hot lights) and so on. (By the way, there are a million tricks to making food look good, including stamping sear marks on meat that is virtually raw to make it look cooked and tasty in the final ad, and using special formulas that mimic the texture of ice cream but don't melt under megawatt lights.)

Traffic

The traffic department is responsible for making sure that an ad meets its deadline. It does this by smoothing the flow of materials from one department to another. Once the "work order" (the go-ahead to start an ad) is given, the traffic department is responsible for finding out when the ad is scheduled to run. For example, the traffic department might find out from the media department (more about media to follow) that a print ad is scheduled to run in *Ladies' Home Journal.* Every magazine has a "close date" for each issue; for most magazines the close is generally about six weeks to two months before the magazine actually hits the newsstands. For example, the May issue of a magazine, which hits the newsstands in mid- to late-April, might close its ad pages on March 1. The traffic department works backward from that date, and many others if the client is using a broad variety of media, to determine the schedule that the production of the ad will have to follow: when production of a television ad needs to be completed (that would include the time needed to edit the tape or do any transfers), when an illustration, photography or color separations would have to be completed, etc.

Trafficking is a very detail-oriented job, especially when one considers that some advertisers have literally hundreds of ads running every day. The **production department** of an agency that handles a major airline account, for example, might have to churn out several hundred ads a day to conform with different fares in each city newspaper in which it advertises, as well as the different specifications (*e.g.,* dimensions of the ad, preparation of photographs and illustrations) of each newspaper for, say, a half-page ad. And since the traffic department is running interference with literally every function within an agency, this can be a very stressful job. It requires a strong, level-headed and diplomatic person to do it well.

Media

Simply put, the media department is in charge of planning and purchasing time on broadcast stations (television or radio), or space in print outlets (magazines or newspapers) and other media, such as billboards.

In the old days, **media buyers** and **media planners** were considered by many as little more than number crunchers, since much of the job was and is involved with deciding how to get the best advertising "buys." But as the sheer number of media outlets has increased over the years, the media buyer's job has become more and more creative. Media buyers and planners today must decide not only what is the most attractive buy for a client from the standpoint of money, but also which is the smartest buy for actually reaching the product's target audience. In the 1980s media buyers and planners finally received much of the respect they had always deserved.

Within agencies, there are two basic types of jobs: the media planner and the media buyer. The media planner is responsible for deciding, with the client, the account executive and the research department, which media outlets will be used for advertising. For example, for a large car company, a media planner might decide that television is the best place to run ads, because the planner wants to cast a wide net and hit as many viewers as possible. For a product such as an industrial-strength insecticide, the planner might be more likely to choose a trade magazine for farmers.

A number of elements come into play when making this decision:

- who the advertising is targeted to
- whether or not the product is seasonal
- what the budget is

This last consideration is extremely important. Although television, for example, is certainly the sexiest media to use, only the biggest media budgets can accommodate the cost of national TV exposure. However, savvy media planners and buyers know plenty of tricks: Though a national TV spot may be out of the question, a "spot TV" buy—one that runs only in local or regional markets—may allow a client to use TV at a substantial savings over a national TV buy.

In some agencies the media planner is also responsible for print buys. The media buyer, on the other hand, concentrates on broadcast buys on radio and TV and sometimes is known as a **broadcast buyer**.

Once the basic decision about media is made, media buyers are the people who actually choose specifically what TV stations or magazines within that category will be used. Number crunching is a certain part of their job, since media buyers must decide which vehicles are most cost-efficient. But the job of media buyer is no longer just crunching numbers. The savvy media buyer is also so involved in knowing who the target audience is that he or she might decide to go with an offbeat TV show that will hit the target audience.

The changing face of television has complicated the job of a media buyer in recent years. Years ago, there were really only a limited number of choices when it came to television—buying "national time" or "spot time"—that is, in TV the so-called "Big Three" networks (NBC, CBS and ABC) were the only game around. This has changed dramatically. In the 1980s a fourth network, Fox, emerged and succeeded in taking audience share away from the networks. "Superstations" such as Atlanta's WTBS and Chicago's WGN broadcast all over the country. Likewise, cable television, which is now available in about 54 percent of the country's households, made real inroads. In fact, the situation for the three major networks has gotten so bad that, in 1989, in a workshop held by the Association of National Advertisers, the heads of the Big Three acknowledged for the first time that their grip on the prime-time audience, which was hovering at 68 percent, would drop into the mid-50s in the next decade. Taken together, these developments represent a major change in the way Americans watch television.

The invention of remote-control devices also figures into a media buyer's calculations. These have created a whole new species of television viewers—couch potatoes known as "zappers" who use the device to "zap" to another program when a station break comes on the program they are watching. It is hardly reassuring to an advertiser who has spent $25,000 for 30 seconds of television time to find out that a large segment of his audience has "zapped" the spot. The result? Shorter commercials—the new norm seems to be fifteen seconds—are being produced in an effort to capture the audience's attention.

The increased use of VCR's has also cut into the television advertiser's pie. As more and more Americans use the machines to catch up on a movie that they didn't have time to see in the theater or at its normal viewing time, it usually means time taken away from watching TV shows and their ads. Likewise, those who have taped television shows for later viewing are using remote-control devices to fast-forward through commercials. This hasn't escaped the notice of the largest TV advertisers. Ads are beginning to encroach upon home videos, and some advertisers are trying to create ads that are so attention-getting, even at fast-forward, that a zapper would want to stop zapping and take a look.

All these elements put a lot of pressure on advertising media departments, as does the increasing number of companies that provides the media-buying service for large clients. Since the 15 percent commission charge by agencies for placing media is usually its biggest source of revenue, media departments must always prove they are making the smartest buys. This is particularly true given the increasing use of "lowballing." For a large advertiser, taking 5 or 8 percent off that 15 percent amounts to huge savings. Many clients have also created their own in-house agencies and media-buying companies as another way to save the 15 percent commission.

As the number of advertising agencies willing to work for less than 15 percent increases, so does the ability of the media buyer to get television time and print space for less than the standard rate. Indeed, the best buyers are usually the best negotiators, able to get a lower price for a 30-second television commercial than a more inexperienced buyer. There are a number of factors that determine whether a buyer can get a lower rate, not the least of which is the clout of the advertiser for whom he or she is working. Giant clients such as R.J. Reynolds, Coca-Cola and Procter & Gamble, for instance, because they spend millions of dollars on advertising every year, would be more likely to command a lower rate than a small, one-time-only national advertiser.

On the print side, the situation has changed as well. There has emerged a plethora of publications targeted to a smaller and smaller audience, which caused one media buyer to surmise that someday the audience would get so specifically targeted that there would be a publication called *Nineteen-Year-Old Unemployed Secretary.* Although he meant it in jest, the truth of the matter is that publications are indeed becoming more directly targeted.

Several other factors have made the jobs of media buyers more complicated. Because of competition, many publications have gone "off the rate card," or "off the card," which lists the standard prices for different advertising units (a page, or half page, in color or black-and-white). In other words, even though a four-color page in a magazine is supposed to go for $4,000, a magazine may go off the card for a cheaper rate in special circumstances, *e.g.,* wanting to lure in a new advertiser. Although discounts have always been common for advertisers who buy multiple pages, in the 1980s even bigger discounts were not uncommon in a variety of situations.

Research

Research is another agency function that underwent much change in the 1980s. The biggest change was that many agencies, looking to cut costs, decided to phase out their research divisions and rely instead on independent research companies. But whether agencies use their own in-house department or an outside service, research is one of the most important departments in helping clients decide whom their target audiences are and how best to reach them.

Market research is used to determine who the buyer of a product generally is, how these buyers feel about the product and its competition and an endless array of other pertinent information on consumer likes and dislikes. The researcher either gets this information from a customized research survey, from other available databases or from the client itself, in the case of a new product. One technique often used to determine how consumers feel about a product and its advertising is to organize "focus groups," which usually work as follows:

Awards are the way that many agencies size up how they are doing creatively. But with the proliferation of awards shows—at last count there were more than 300, from general shows for national advertising to those honoring the best farm equipment commercials—it seemed to some that virtually every agency was winning awards. In 1988 *Adweek's Winner's* magazine sought to cut through the ad-show clutter. It polled creatives all over the country to determine the top shows in terms of prestige and difficulty. The results:

- The One Show
- Cannes
- The New York Art Directors Show
- Communication Arts magazine's awards
- British Design and Art Direction
- Stephen F. Kelly
- Clios
- The New York Festivals
- Andys (awarded by the New York Ad Club)
- Effies (American Marketing Association)
- Addies (The American Advertising Federation)

Using these awards as a guide, *Winner's* determined that the top 10 agencies were, in order:

- Fallon McElligott
- Chiat/Day
- BBDO
- Hal Riney & Partners
- Ogilvy & Mather
- Levine, Huntley Schmidt & Beaver
- The Martin Agency
- Hill, Holliday, Connors, Cosmopoulos
- DDB Needham
- Foote, Cone & Belding

A trained leader talks to a group of consumers who fit the product's target profile about how they feel about the product. Often this is done in specially equipped rooms in which agency personnel sit on one side of a two-way mirror so they can observe the focus group without actually being in the same room.

Information from these gatherings is then sorted through by the account, research and creative teams to determine what the advertising strategy should be. If a focus group was asked about a laundry product, for example, it would likely consist of homemakers in the twenty-five-to-forty-year-old age group. If, during the course of their discussion, some of the home-makers commented that they would like a detergent that made their clothes both white and soft, the creative team might decide to play up the "softness" virtue in the ad campaign. The focus group conversation might also elicit the feeling that previous advertising campaigns talked down to these home-makers.

Then, equipped with this information, creative teams and account executives can continue trying to decide on the advertising strategy.

Focus groups are useful primarily because they provide marketers with information beyond the hard numbers of qualitative research to show not only that people are more inclined to buy product A over product B, but why they are more attracted to product A.

Observing groups of consumers in this manner doesn't come cheap. Depending on the facilities used, payment of the moderators and the participants can easily run from $2,500 to $4,000. If the product that the focus group is being asked about is "upscale," the cost might well be higher, because the consumers who are interviewed are likely to be busy professionals whose time would cost the agency more.

There are several keys to using focus groups effectively, and there are ways the information they provide can be abused. One crucial step is to use a moderator who asks the proper questions without "leading" the respondents. The best moderators will stick to the "discussion guide" (which is prepared by the agency, perhaps with some input from the client, and covers the information needed by the client), but will also be flexible enough to allow the focus group to edge over into other areas, if it seems that this might provide useful information to the client.

The techniques used to get information from the focus group include projective techniques—word-association games, flash cards or flip sheets—requiring respondents to complete sentences about the product. Some research methods are fairly elaborate. For instance, a mock-supermarket aisle, complete with an array of products, might be created and used to study in-store behavior. "Consumers" would be asked to "buy" products and then explain their "purchases." Did the packaging appeal to them? Was price a factor? Did the shelf placement help them make a decision?

One factor that often interferes with an effective focus group is having a bossy individual who takes over the group and dominates the conversation. On the other end of the spectrum is the participant who is only too eager to please, and seems to say whatever he or she thinks the moderator wants to hear. The information received from either of these individuals hurts the chances of getting valid, unbiased, truly representative information from the focus group.

Focus groups are best used to determine specific reactions by consumers, for example, to the specific language used in an ad. Focus groups are also helpful in leading researchers to areas that might need redefinition. For example, sometimes the process of product development omits a crucial consideration. One company wanted to introduce what it thought was a new and improved way of baking cakes—adding water to an already prepared mix. It wasn't until the focus groups spoke that the company ran up against a fact it had overlooked—that when it comes to baking consumers wanted to feel as if they'd done at least a little work, and adding water just wasn't enough. The new, lab-created method was too convenient, and it took a focus group to discover why!

Some new focus-group techniques force consumers to decide what is most important about a product, showing not only what they want but also how badly they want it. For instance, consumers may be asked if they're willing to spend

Advertising Agencies Aren't the Only Places Where There Are Jobs Having to Do with Advertising.

You can also work for a television station, or a radio network or a newspaper or magazine, and get experience from the media side selling "space" for advertisements. Ad salespeople deal frequently with agency media people. While the latter are trying to get the best positioning and the best deals for the agency and advertiser, ad salespeople are trying to get the most money for the space they have to offer while at the same time trying to develop long-standing relationships with clients. Obviously, there is ample room for bargaining. This give-and-take—and the ability to attract new business—is what makes or breaks a good advertising salesperson. In fact, their jobs are often "incentivized" to reward their acumen and tenacity out in the field.

To get experience from the client side, there are an increasing number of jobs available at "in-house" advertising or marketing departments. These are most often formed to cut down on the cost of hiring outside expertise,

10, 25 or even 50 percent more than what the current competition charges.

The smartest marketers realize that there are many regional differences in consumer tastes that must be taken into consideration. In the case of a chewing-tobacco product, an agency and client based in New York City would be smart to seek out focus groups in rural areas in order to get information from consumers who might be more likely to use the product.

In recent years, it has become common to "pre-test" advertising in front of another group of consumers to see how they react before lots of money is spent on the actual production.

but in fact no one knows a company's business as well as its own people. The jobs here are pretty much the same as at an ad agency—copywriters, creative directors, researchers, traffic managers, etc. Companies also have people in charge of local co-op advertising—advertising that is done in conjunction with local retailers and vendors. Companies who do hire ad agencies to perform these functions need a person (or persons) to oversee the agency's work to make sure the agency is creating effective advertising. This is an extremely demanding job, and an excellent way to gain quick exposure to the full realm of agency work.

There is a great deal of job switching within these areas. An agency copywriter might become a company's director of advertising. The media person at a TV station might join an advertising agency as a media buyer. And so on. There are also the financial people following in the footsteps of the Saatchis and Martin Sorrell, making their mark in the business side of the field before coming to prominence as VIPs in charge of vast advertising holding companies. What it all boils down to is this: When it comes to the advertising business, there is a career path for everyone.

In the case of print ads this is done in rough sketches that give the gist and flavor of the final ad without the photography or illustrations. In the case of TV ads, the creative team is likely to use "storyboards," which are art boards in which one frame from each scene of the TV spot has been drawn, with accompanying copy underneath. To improve the chances of consumers' understanding what the finished commercial will look like, some agencies resort to what is called "steal-o-matics"—that is, taking existing footage from TV programs or other spots and splicing them together to form a rough simulation.

As might be expected, creative teams normally loathe pretesting ads, and even feel equally disdainful of the information that is provided by focus groups. Though most creatives would agree that information provided before they begin the creative process helps decide what to include and what to avoid, most creatives have a real problem with using groups to evaluate advertising, particularly when the groups are shown only roughs of print ideas or storyboards. Creatives argue that many subtleties that come with the finished versions are persuasive and crucial to how the ads are perceived by consumers. By the same token, creatives argue that summoning groups to give their opinions before the campaign is too far along kills many good ideas prematurely.

Account Planners

In some American agencies, a relatively new job function called **account planning** has come into vogue. Although this position has long been used in British agencies, it came into fashion with U.S agencies only in the 1980s. Basically, an account planner falls somewhere in between the account executive and an agency researcher.

In essence, the account planner is something of an agency advocate for the consumer. He is taught to think like a consumer. He goes out and actually meets consumers, in shopping centers, stores, malls—wherever consumers gather to consume. In a way, this is an extension of the research function, but it is interpretive rather than statistical. The account planner gives his research and impressions directly with the creative team.

Chiat/Day is one of the American agencies that uses the account-planning function. Agency founder Jay Chiat has said that he believes having someone to represent the consumer through all phases of the creative process is conducive to getting the best and most effective work.

Other Agency Roles

Though job descriptions vary from agency to agency, at some of the largest American shops it is not unheard of to have a full-time **curator** for art on the staff, or a person whose only job is to consult and advise on the use of type (this is another imported British idea, so new, in fact, that there is yet a title for it). Some agencies have a person in the creative department known as the **art buyer** whose only job is to purchase photography and illustrations for the ads.

While at larger agencies job descriptions tend to be more narrow, at smaller shops it is much more common to have creatives who fill more than one function, or traffic people who are jacks-of-all-trades. In fact, as the advertising business becomes more and more consolidated through mergers and acquisitions, that will become truer of the larger agencies as well.

As the advertising world moves closer and closer to more multinational shops, the smart agency employee exercising simple survival instincts should learn as much as possible about other functions within the agency environment.

Chapter **6**

ALTERNATIVE ADVERTISING

I n the late 1980s, "alternative advertising" became as important to advertising agencies and clients as mass advertising. What exactly is alternative advertising? It's a general term for all the different types of media that are more narrow in their focus than "broadcasting," which gets its name simply because it reaches many consumers in one shot.

If you are introducing a new product that has a broad audience, and you have a good budget, TV broadcasting (*e.g.,* placing ads on one of the "Big Three" networks) is usually a smart buy. But if your budget isn't quite as large as you would like, alternative media, also called "narrowcasting," is probably the answer.

Narrowcasting means sending your message to a small but very well defined group of consumers who make up your target audience. There are a number of ways to do this:

- direct marketing
- cable TV
- promotions
- sponsorships of special events or sports competitions

Whittle Communications: Media Maverick

The best example of how alternative media can be used creatively and effectively is provided by Whittle Communications, the Knoxville-based company that has been a fount of new ideas that play off traditional media and succeed at targeting certain audiences more specifically.

Even before forming Whittle Communications, Christopher Whittle had achieved success with targeting specific audiences with special publications. His *Nutshell* magazine, founded in the early 1970s and targeted at incoming freshmen at the nation's colleges and universities, gave birth to the "single-advertiser magazine." This meant that only one company's ads appeared, thereby granting that company not just access to the lucrative teen market but uncluttered access—there were no competitive ads in sight! It was this success that led Whittle to conclude that conventional media just didn't do the proper targeting job for advertisers.

Whittle went on to purchase and resurrect successfully *Esquire* magazine before returning to the realm of alternative media. In 1988 and 1989, he came up with three new types of media that have proved to be very savvy and very controversial.

SPECIAL REPORT

Special Report magazines represent Whittle's attempt to target another influential consumer group—the nation's mothers. Where in the course of a mother's or homemaker's busy day could an advertiser "get hold of" them? Whittle reasoned that a doctor's waiting room, with an average waiting time of about twenty to thirty minutes and an already existing tradition of reading magazines, was as good a place as any. He created *Special Report* magazines in six categories—personalities, sports, health, fiction, living and families—designed to be read in under an hour.

His pitch to advertisers was appealing: category exclusivity, meaning that there would be no competition or clutter. His pitch to doctors was equally persuasive: They would receive the magazines free, plus a handsome display case, provided they limited other waiting-room subscriptions to just two. This last aspect of the program outraged the magazine industry. Magazines count doctors among their most valued subscribers, and some industry people claimed Whittle's restrictions constituted an assault on the U.S. Constitution's freedom of speech guarantees. Whittle's reply was that this was the predictable response of an entrenched, unimaginative industry that had ceased servicing its advertisers. Evidently, advertisers agreed: *Special Report* sold out its advertising space within a month after the project was announced.

"CHANNEL ONE"

"Channel One" was Whittle's idea for targeting high-school students, who are a very lucrative market for many products, such as colas, jeans, candy and even certain types of movies. Many marketers of teen-aged products are willing to pay a premium price to be guaranteed that teen-agers will see their message. However, these teen-agers are increasingly hard for advertisers to target, particularly because they are bombarded by a number of broadcast images, but also because there are very few media geared specifically toward them.

"Channel One" is a short, informational television show of about ten minutes' duration that is designed to bring teens up to date about the news and world issues. In an effort to keep their interest, it is hosted by teen-agers and is produced with the high-tech images teens are used to seeing on shows like MTV (Music Television). Interspersed with the news are commercials. As with Whittle magazines, a product category is sold exclusively, so if Coke buys a spot on the show, that is the only cola ad the teens see. The number of commercials per program is also limited.

The controversial part of this program is that Whittle planned to have the show broadcast in the nation's schools—

in exchange for $50,000 worth of electronic equipment such as VCR's, monitors and satellite dishes. After a testing period that saw an extremely vocal, nationwide debate over the merits of the program, Whittle began his attempts to take the show national. In June 1989 the New York State Board of Regents rejected the program's use, saying that commercial television had no place in the classroom. Others argued that this was a good opportunity for financially troubled schools to get equipment that could be used for other purposes as well. Still others argued that teens are already so accustomed to looking at commercials that two minutes more wouldn't make much of a difference. As of mid-1989, with similar but non-commercial efforts being mounted, it was unclear how Whittle would fare.

ADVERTISING IN BOOKS

Yet another controversial Whittle idea is that of advertising in books. Books once carried advertisements, but the Whittle wrinkle is more prominent. He signed a select group of top authors to write short books about contemporary topics, and paid them handsomely to do so. The books were to be distributed were free of charge to an exclusive, demographically appealing list of national business leaders, government figures and others. Here, too, critics, including many publishers, charged Whittle with perverting a sacred institution in quest of advertising dollars. Others likened the effort to magazines that carry advertising that appears adjacent to articles.

Christopher Whittle is an original thinker, and there is no question that he is full of ideas that are ripe for today's advertising environment—which is becoming more and more inclined to use non-traditional media.

Direct Marketing

Direct marketing is advertising that is targeted to specific individuals and delivered to homes primarily through the mail. It also involves marketers' use of the 800 telephone number so that a prospective customer can call toll-free and order the merchandise directly. The proliferation of home-shopping networks proves the success of this method.

How do you figure out which consumers to target, if you want them to buy, say, an expensive type of chocolates by mail? The first step is to see if there is already a ready-made database available. For example, there are several magazines whose focus is directed entirely to chocolate lovers, so it would be worthwhile to buy their mailing lists, if they are for sale. (Some magazines do not sell their mailing lists.) Otherwise, one might use a tried and true method, such as advertising with coupons in an upscale food magazine such as *Gourmet*. For other products, such as car accessories, it would be easier to find a database, because you can use car registrations, which tell you not only how old the consumer's vehicle is, but what model it is, making it possible for you to refine the message.

As direct marketing becomes more and more important, a growing number of advertising agencies employ people—and sometimes entire departments and subsidiaries—who specialize in direct marketing matters.

Promotion

Promotion is another way for advertisers and agencies to target an audience specifically. Sometimes promotion involves tie-ins with other companies, but frequently it is simply an event or program that draws attention to the product.

For many years promotion was a stepchild to advertising. Broadcast-television advertising and print were considered much sexier, and therefore more fun to work on. But in the 1980s promotion and direct marketing came into their own, and smart agencies now consider a pamphlet or coupon just as important as a print ad. Smart clients treat these projects as an important part of their sum-total marketing effort, even though they sometimes cost substantially less than a broadcast effort.

"Special-events marketing" is an area of promotion that grew by leaps and bounds in the 1980s. The use of popular musical groups to promote a product is one of the biggest areas of growth. Pepsi signed Michael Jackson as an endorser and sponsored the Jacksons's Victory Tour. For its $5 million, Pepsi got the Jacksons to do two TV spots, and its name appeared on all concert tickets. It also got the use of signage in some of the stadiums where the tour played, but not all of them: Coke has exclusive year-round signage rights to many of the stadiums in the United States, and it was not about to give them up to Pepsi for this very hot ticket.

Pepsi also signed Lionel Richie quick on the heels of reeling in Michael Jackson. Coke in turn signed Julio Iglesias for a fee rumored at $10 million. From there it turned into a free-for-all. Coke signed Robert Palmer; Pepsi got Madonna. (Her spots, which used the same music as her video, which featured religious imagery and an assault on a woman, were eventually pulled.) Beer marketers got into the game with music stars, too. Michelob signed Eric Clapton and Steve Winwood.

What does a marketer get for all these astronomical expenditures? Usually, a couple of TV spots featuring the star, the use of the star at press conferences, ads for local tie-ins at each place the star plays, signage at the stadium and its name on the concert tickets. It also gets a measure of prestige, if the star is red-hot. The good will created by sponsoring a tour and a hot star is unmeasurable. Sometimes controversy of one form or another descends upon a star who has been signed for commercial use, but since this is a relatively rare occurrence, advertisers seem willing to take the risk of negative publicity or wasted money.

Not surprisingly, the more hesitant a star is to sponsor a product, the more alluring he or she is to advertisers. Bruce Springsteen's "Born in the USA" anthem was something one advertiser wanted so badly for his car company that he offered $10 million for the part of the song that used those words. Springsteen declined.

Music is not the only form of special-event marketing. Philip Morris pushes its Marlboro cigarettes via sponsorship of race cars on the Indy car circuit as a way to get its name out in front of the public. Since cigarette advertising has been banned from television for more than two decades, cigarette advertisers are always looking for promotional vehicles like this. Marlboro has its own racing team, which is the cornerstone of its Marlboro Motorsports program. The company sponsors two cars, which have the Marlboro name painted on them, as well as two major events on the CART/PPG circuit—the Marlboro Gran Prix and the Marlboro 500.

Special-events marketing includes all other sports as well—tennis is a major event for many tennis manufacturers. Have you ever noticed how most major tennis stars have a small label sewn on their shirt-sleeve (sometimes more than one)? These are emblems of tennis manufacturers or other companies who have paid the athlete money to be a sponsor. In return they get their name on the athletes' outfit; a form of advertising whose effectiveness is nearly impossible to evaluate. But since the athlete is on the screen almost constantly, the advertiser can be assured that it is getting name recognition and reinforcement with the target audience.

Other ways advertisers can gain awareness for their products is to stage a tie-in promotion with a special event. For example, if an advertiser was one of the sponsors of the Olympic games, it might stage a sweepstakes or game promotion. For a food company like McDonald's, the game pieces could be given away at the restaurant. For a big company like Coca-Cola, consumers could pick up the necessary playing pieces at supermarkets and convenience stores.

Special events such as the Olympics provide a number of options for the advertiser who has deep pockets. Sometimes sports events will sell product exclusivity for certain categories, such as colas, fast food or camera companies. This exclusivity comes at a price, but a huge audience for such events usually makes it worthwhile for the advertiser. The networks generally make a promise about how large the viewing audience will be, and if the numbers slip below that guarantee, they will give the advertiser a "make-good"—that is, a promise of free ad time on a future program.

For events like the Olympics, advertisers are occasionally

allowed to lock in on one sport, like skating or gymnastics. This is a way for an advertiser to use broadcasting while actually narrowcasting to a very specific audience—those interested in that particular sport.

> "There is no such thing as national advertising. All advertising is local and personal. It's one man or woman reading one newspaper in the kitchen or watching TV in the den."
>
> —Morris Hite, in *Adman*

Special events also are a good way for advertisers to target ethnic groups. Miller Lite, in 1989, signed an agreement to sponsor the band La Mafia™ as a way to target the emerging Hispanic market. The sponsorship included appearances by the band in television and radio spots for Miller Lite, including participation in Miller's regional ad campaign that features actor Randy Quaid. La Mafia will also receive promotional support from Miller for the band's 100-plus appearance dates each year of the contract.

What are some examples of the top promotions of 1988? Six companies created innovative promotions that won *Promote* magazine's Second Annual Event Marketing Awards. The Grand Prize went to the Georgia-Pacific Corporation for its "The World's Fastest Roofer Contest." To show roofing contractors all of the G-P products, the contest concluded with a roofer winning an all-expenses-paid trip to Hawaii for being the fastest roofer and the one most concerned with job quality. The contest started with 150 roofers in eight regional centers. Georgia-Pacific increased its single sales in target markets by 90 percent with the promotion, an outstanding success.

Other winners were:

- MTV's Museum of Un-Natural History, an exhibit that featured an interplay of rock and roll, style, fashion and technology

- The Sundance™ Grand Prix of Cycling, sponsored by Stroh Foods Inc., a six-city series of cycling races designed to give Olympic cyclists some special competitions before the big race, and to promote Stroh's new non-alcoholic, juice-based drinks

- "The Adults-Only Peanut Butter Lovers Fan Club Reunion," a four-day reunion to boost consumption of peanut butter by adults, sponsored by the Peanut Advisory Board

- "The Old-Style River Raft Race," sponsored by G. Heileman Brewing Inc., a series of charity-related raft races in Chicago, Illinois, and in Milwaukee and Madison, Wisconsin

- "The Friskiest Cats in America" contest, sponsored by The Carnation Co., a contest to find the friskiest cat in America, which included a tie-in with *Cat Fancy* magazine and a calendar featuring photos of the winning cat

Alternative advertising, seen by a prescient view a few years ago as the wave of the future, has arrived.

Chapter 7

TRUTH IN ADVERTISING

ruth be told, members of the advertising profession rank just above used-car salesmen in terms of how little they are trusted. And, admittedly, it's sometimes easy to see why, when the following tactics are standard for the trade:

• hawking a product or service as "new and improved" when really it offers nothing new

• "bait and switch" car advertisements, in which a car is advertised in its most stripped-down version so that the sales person can later talk the consumer into purchasing something more expensive

Such tactics have done little to boost the trust of the American public in the advertising business. Indeed, much of the public regards ads as outright lies. From the industry point of view, it is the unscrupulous few who taint things for the professional many. Whatever the case, "truth in advertising" remains an important issue of public debate, and there exists a variety of checks and balances on the ads the public sees.

65

The Role of Government

During the Reagan years, the federal government became more disinclined to police the claims made in advertisements. However, others moved in to fill that role—state legislators eager to gain additional revenues from a new idea known as an ad tax, and consumer activists just doing their job.

Still, the first place an ad is judged as to its truthfulness is through several branches of government. The two biggest enforcers of advertising activity are the Federal Trade Commission (FTC) and the Federal Communications Commission (FCC).

The FTC monitors advertising and also is the place where consumer complaints about unfair and deceptive ads are lodged. The FTC can issue a "cease and desist" order to advertisers and agencies that it has found using untrue ads.

The FCC has control over television and radio stations—what they are allowed to broadcast, and how many hours a day are given over to certain kinds of programming. The FCC also holds stations responsible for the advertising they air, which has made some TV stations force advertisers to substantiate claims, particularly competitive claims, before the ads are actually run. This means that stations can make calls about ads that they consider questionable (most frequently these are any—such as for condoms or feminine-hygiene products—that have a sexual connotation, even if remotely so). Most networks have censors, but their ranks have been cut as a cost-saving maneuver; that's why risqué material is more likely these days to make it to your TV screens—the censors who are left simply can't police everything. Likewise, for the same reason, one commercial may make it through one station's bureaucracy and not another.

Government regulation can have many effects, some of them potentially devasting for advertisers wanting to get their message to the large number of people reached through broadcasting. It was the government's ruling that cigarette-smoking is harmful to one's health that caused the ban of cigarette advertising on television. Today, ads for cigarettes, once one of the largest product categories to use TV advertising, are seen only on billboards and in magazines and newspapers.

For similar reasons, alcoholic products are never actually consumed on TV commercials. You may think you've seen characters in TV ads drink, but in fact they never do. Through a kind of sleight of hand, agencies show characters being refreshed after having a sip, but never the sip itself. One ad, for an Australian beer, actually spoofs the prohibition by having actor Paul Hogan telling the camera to hurry up and fade to black so he can have a taste of the beer he's hawking.

Alcohol manufacturers may not be laughing for very much longer. Many legislators have targeted alcohol advertising as the next big category that should be limited in the kind of ads it can run. Not surprisingly, alcohol advertisers are fighting this limitation, but some legislators are determined to try at least to ban alcohol ads from television, where they feel it influences young people to drink.

Public Watchdogs

Probably the biggest group that monitors false and deceptive advertising is the National Advertising Division of the Council for Better Business Bureaus. NAD receives complaints from advertisers and agencies, and forces them either to prove the points made in ads or withdraw them.

Most often the kinds of complaints that are brought before NAD have to do with comparative advertising, in which one product claims superiority over another. For example, if one brand of deodorant is purported to be 52 percent more effective than another, the advertiser and agency would have to bring out test results or some other type of proof to demonstrate that the claim was legitimate. Sometimes the tests themselves are not enough. NAD can decide that the tests were carried out in a biased way, for example, by forcing consumers to have no choice but to pick one product over another.

Because of the problems involved in comparative advertising, and because that form of advertising is being used more and more, many agencies keep a legal person either on staff or on retainer as a consultant in order to avoid having problems with substantiating claims.

Children's Advertising

Advertising targeted at children is another area that is policed by activist groups. Legislators, mindful of protecting an impressionable audience, and much to the chagrin of advertisers, are constantly introducing bills that would cut back on the amount of advertising that can run per hour of children's programming, particularly during Saturday-morning cartoon shows.

The self-appointed watchdog of anything having to do with children and advertising is a group called Action for Children's Television. Founded in 1968 by homemaker Peggy Charren, ACT was created in order to improve the quality of programming targeted toward children, while at the same time limit the influence of deceptive advertising. Charren's group has been one of the most vocal about TV shows that are based on commercially-sold toys, feeling that it is almost brainwashing children who are too young to differentiate their favorite TV show from an ad. The group has also been very critical of Whittle Communications's "Channel One" (see page 58), because they feel that advertisements for commercial products have no place in schools, where objective learning is the practice and goal.

ACT has had its ups and downs. It succeeded in getting Congress to pass legislation limiting the amount of advertising on Saturday-morning television, traditionally the highest viewing time for children. Previously there were no such restrictions. However, one of Ronald Reagan's last acts as president was to veto a bill, which grew out of an ACT suit, that would have further limited the amount of commercial time during children's broadcasts. It is believed that Reagan's action was

The Ad Tax

Advertisers and advertising agencies are accustomed to being the targets of abuse. Now they're under attack from another quarter—those who want to tax what they do.

Although there are currently no ad taxes, many states, their budgets suffering, have tried to institute a tax in order to increase revenues. In 1988, no fewer than six states offered legislation to tax advertising.

In 1987, Florida became the first state to pass such a law, much to the surprise of advertising agencies and advertisers all over the country. However, the state of Florida quickly found out that enforcing such a tax was nearly impossible. Who was to be taxed—the agencies creating ads for clients that were out of state, or Florida clients only? What was to be done about magazines with ads that were produced in other states and mailed into Florida? In just a few months, the outroar in the ad community, stoked by a huge rally at the national convention of the American Advertising Federation in Tampa, helped get the tax repealed. The AAF and the Association of National Advertisers argued successfully in court that such a law was a violation of free speech and therefore illegal. Still, that ruling hasn't dissuaded several other states from trying the same thing.

Connecticut also tried to institute a tax on advertising. In May 1988, the opponents of such a tax claimed victory when the governor signed into law a service tax bill that excluded media-related advertising services. Meanwhile, the Texas Legislature adjourned in 1989 without considering an ad tax for the first time since the threat emerged in 1984. Other states frequently have ad-tax legislation introduced. Industry observers expect much turmoil on this front in the 1990s.

motivated by his well-known reluctance to regulate commercial enterprise.

Other Groups

Perhaps encouraged by the visibility of groups such as ACT, and dismayed by the federal government's lack of interest in policing programming, several grass-roots consumer groups targeted television advertising in the 1980s. Perhaps the best known is a group headed by the Rev. Donald Wildmon, a Mississippi minister who started Christian Leaders for Responsible Television. This group had only limited success in the early 1980s, but in 1988 Wildmon's group gained new power as it threatened boycotts of advertisers on shows that it found offensive. In a similar vein, in 1989 a single individual, Terry Rakolta, a Bloomfield Hills, Michigan homemaker, went up against major advertisers who had purchased time on a program she found offensive, the Fox network's "Married with Children." Rakolta had been miffed at the show's sexual overtones and the fact that such programming was aired early in the evening, a time when it could be seen by kids. (The independent Fox network is not bound by the Big Three's "family programming" commitment, which mandates the kind of shows that can be aired at certain times of the day.) She succeeded in having advertisers pull their ads from future broadcasts of the show. Emboldened by this action, Rakolta started a group called Americans for Responsible Television. ART planned to ask the top 100 advertisers in the United States for information about the criteria they use in choosing programming for their ads, and to issue a report on what programming these advertisers sponsor and have refused to sponsor. Johnson & Johnson and Wendy's were two of the companies that provided ART with the guidelines.

For many consumers, truth in advertising is the main issue. The pervasiveness of advertising in our society is a virtual guarantee that attempts will continue to make sure advertising does its job fairly and squarely .

Chapter 8

BURGER KING: ADVERTISING THE HARD WAY

Having one of the nation's largest advertising budgets does not necessarily guarantee success. The case of Burger King, the Miami-based fast-food company, exemplifies this advertising maxim. Burger King's annual advertising budget weighs in at over $200 million. When you add in all the millions that are also contributed to advertising by local cooperatives—groupings of local Burger King franchises and local businesses who also advertise—you have a company with major advertising and marketing muscle.

Still, in the 1970s and 1980s, Burger King has found out the hard way that big bucks do not automatically translate into big sales. Indeed, many marketing lessons can be learned from what this company has done over the years. True, Burger King did manage, for a time, to make some inroads on market leader McDonald's. But then, through a series of faulty strategy decisions and major personnel shakeups within Burger King and its marketing staff, the company found itself struggling just to maintain the status quo.

In the beginning, at least, Burger King seemed to be on track. In the 1970s, Burger King smartly followed one advertising rule of thumb: If a category of products (*e.g.,* hamburgers) is seen as having parity, and your product is indeed different, the smart client exploits this difference. Burger King did this with advertising that showed how its hamburgers were flame broiled, while McDonald's were fried. The company was also smart enough to promote another attribute that stood in contrast to McDonald's—namely, that at Burger King you could come in and "have it your way." In other words, if you hated pickles, or onions, or wanted a burger plain, with no dressing, you could simply say so when placing your order and Burger King would comply. McDonald's hamburgers, on the other hand, came in one or a few uniform ways, already dressed, forcing customers to scrape off the offending condiment. McDonald's "special grill" took some three to five minutes extra to prepare—a lifetime when you are talking about fast food. Though it might seem that scraping off an offending pickle would be small potatoes in the grand scheme of things, the strategy to position Burger King as the place where you could get a choice was a stroke of genius in the $25 billion fast-food marketplace.

In the 1970s, Burger King's advertising also included a character called the Burger King, a fantasy figure designed to appeal to kids and to counteract the magic of McDonald's popular Ronald McDonald.™ This was also a smart move, for several reasons. Kids are very influential when it comes to persuading Mom and Dad which fast-food restaurant they want to patronize. Families of three and four make up a huge market for fast-food companies, much more so than single adults. This means spending more per visit, too. Industry statistics and polls show that about 38 percent of adults aged eighteen and over visit fast-food restaurants ten times in a three-month period; for families, the percentage is about 45 percent. So getting the attention of kids is very important, to say the least.

Nonetheless, Burger King decided to give up the magical Burger King character in the late 1970s, and has never reinstituted a plan to revive him or introduce a similar character. Why did this happen? One of the reasons is that McDonald's, whose budget of $800 million is almost four times that of Burger King, was spending the same amount on Ronald McDonald commercials that Burger King had in its entire advertising budget, swamping Burger King's attempts to create any lasting identity for its character. Indeed, today the only remnant of the Burger "king" is a paper crown that kids can get in some restaurants.

What followed were years of unrest and turmoil. Though the company used the services of J. Walter Thompson, one of the country's best-known and most-respected ad agencies, there were many false starts and bad strategies.

For one thing, a proliferation of fast-food companies during the 1970s and 1980s confronted Burger King, and other hamburger restaurants, with more competition. These other chains included hamburger outlets such as Wendy's, chicken chains such as Kentucky Fried Chicken and Bojangles,™ seafood restaurants such as Long John Silver, and Mexican-themed restaurants such as Taco Bell.™

Burger King decided that diversification would be a good way to fend off this charge, and the chain introduced a number of specialty sandwiches, such as the Veal Parmigiana. Unfortunately, these kinds of offerings were about as far away from burgers as you could get, and they proved a bad choice for Burger King. The specialty sandwiches were eventually eliminated.

In the 1980s, Burger King introduced another advertising effort called "Aren't You Hungry?" The campaign proved to be a failure because, advertising experts observed, the question was just too broad. "Aren't you hungry?" could be construed to mean "Aren't you hungry for just any fast-food hamburger?," which hardly did anything to differentiate Burger King from its competitors.

Another widespread failure, and probably the company's most visible advertising effort that didn't work, was the 1986 campaign featuring "Herb the Nerd."™ Herb was supposed to be the only person in America who hadn't eaten a Burger King hamburger. The series of rapidly changing TV ads featured the search for this elusive character, the idea being to create some excitement with the ads and with the idea that regular consumers might be able to "catch" Herb. Finally, against the ad agency's recommendations, Herb's identity was revealed: He turned out to be a thirtyish guy who wore glasses and was balding, not exactly the sexy image for which most advertisers and companies strive.

According to a memo issued by J. Walter Thompson to its staff after it lost the account in 1987, the Herb campaign and its mission were misunderstood, even by Burger King's own franchises.

"One of the most talked about, but misunderstood events of 1986 was Herb," said the memo. "Herb was not an advertising campaign—it was never intended to be. In fact, it was never intended at all. Burger King marketing had originally scheduled a hot new product, Chicken Tenders,™ to be launched during this time to help blunt McDonald's launch of the McDLT™ sandwich. When the Chicken Tenders launch was scratched at the last minute, we were faced with six weeks to come up with creative to blunt the million-dollar-a-day spending level McDonald's planned for McDLT, a sandwich which directly threatened the Whopper.™ Herb was created as a promotion, not a campaign." (One similar, but successful, promotion was Miller Beer's "Case of the Missing Case.")

The memo went on: "While admittedly Herb may have been a risk, it was by no means a disaster. In the face of the McDLT launch, sales for Burger King did not decline, while Wendy's sales dipped significantly and awareness of Burger King was at an all-time high. The promotion did accomplish its objective. Until we revealed Herb, the advertising was very well received."

The campaign proved to be an expensive failure, costing Burger King an estimated $40 million.

Yet another campaign was launched later in 1986. This one was called "Burger King Town" and sought to emulate the homey scenes and good feelings that McDonald's has always done so well within its advertising. The ads certainly had a different look: images of "typical" backyard barbecues, shot on

Super-8 film, gave the ads that "home movie" feeling. However, it may have been a case of too little too late, since the campaign did not work the required magic. Observers commented that Burger King, still reeling, was in need of something with a little more "grab."

Next on the agenda was "the best food for fast times." Once again Burger King had changed its strategy, this time deciding that consumers didn't want homespun values but speed instead. This campaign was a strategic mistake. The simple fact of the matter was that customers could walk into a McDonald's and get a burger faster than they could at Burger King, primarily because the Burger King burger was made to order, and the McDonald's burger was ready-made, meaning it was ready to go as soon as patrons ordered it. Consumers knew this, too, and the ads didn't wash. To complement the "fast times" theme—and the idea of being able to eat a hamburger fast—Burger King introduced several new bite-sized versions of its regular hamburger. The whole campaign proved to be a failure, and the ultimate undoing of J. Walter Thompson as well. In 1987, after eleven years with Thompson, Burger King launched an agency review. Although incumbent Thompson was included with the other contenders, the company eventually awarded its account to NW Ayer.

It is something of a tradition in the advertising business that client companies blame their advertising for almost everything that goes wrong. Burger King's relationship with NW Ayer proved that the problems at the company were their own. Ayer's first effort for Burger King returned to the idea that had been the company's most successful to date—that consumers liked the idea of having their burgers broiled rather than fried. The campaign that followed used the tagline "We'd do it like you'd do it," and the ads featured images of consumers broiling burgers out in their backyards, just like Burger King did in its restaurants. In a humorous, creative attack on the competition, Burger King and Ayer also showed people barbecuing in their backyards with giant frying pans!—a nice way to skewer the competition. In another spot, a young man was shown getting out his own specially made hamburgers for his girlfriend, reaching inside the hood of an outdoor smoker to retrieve a bag of Burger King hamburgers. The ads didn't do the trick, however. Sales for the first quarter of 1988 were 3 percent lower than the same period in 1987. Still, the ads were good, leading many to think that the problems lay with Burger King. They did.

In the space of just ten years, Burger King has gone through:

- a management shake-up in which the company's vice-presidents of advertising, marketing and promotions were all ousted
- the buyout of its parent company, Pillsbury, by Grand Metropolitan PLC, which brought in its own management team
- four different marketing managers
- several different presidents
- several different chairmen

This changing management, as much as any one single factor, has kept Burger King from keeping its sights trained and marketing focus steady.

In late 1988 Burger King chose to focus not on a new campaign from NW Ayer but on a number of special promotions (a second Whopper for 35 cents if you bought one, for example). For a time Burger King even revived some of the ads that J. Walter Thompson had created. Finally, eighteen short months after it was hired, NW Ayer found itself in the same boat as J. Walter Thompson—the agency was fired from the $215 million account.

What went wrong? Some of the explanations may be found in the memo that J. Walter Thompson issued after it lost the account. Certain factors "go with the territory in the fast-food business," the memo said:

- a short-term "sales" orientation in perhaps the toughest retail business there is
- a rapidly changing market

- frenetic personnel changes, leaving no consistent direction for the company
- an "incredible competitor in McDonald's, who had us out-gunned by a large margin in marketing dollars and was hell-bent on burying Burger King"

The memo concluded: "These factors do more than anything else to explain the lack of continuity in marketing/advertising programs at Burger King. No agency wants to change campaigns, and we recommended vehemently against this. Unfortunately, we did not always win."

Certainly, there is much to recommend staying with a proven thing. Some campaigns, such as "Rosie the waitress" in commercials for Bounty™ paper towels, Madge the manicurist for Palmolive dishwashing detergent and Mr. Whipple for Charmin™ bathroom tissue have shown that consumers identify with a recurrent character and message. This is one lesson that Burger King did not learn during the 1970s and 1980s.

When Thompson was fired in 1987, it responded with an ad that demonstrated the integrity for which the agency was known. The ad showed a graph of how average store sales for Burger King had increased by 145 percent since J. Walter Thompson took over the account in 1976, and how McDonald's average store sales growth increased only 87 percent during that same period. The ad was, in effect, a pat on the back by J. Walter Thompson management to its employees, but it was also a gracious gesture to Burger King as well. The body copy said simply: "We shared the very best of times and made a lot of friends for life. We wish you every success."

Such good manners surely pay off in the rough-and-tumble world of marketing. After Ayer was fired, Burger King announced the agencies it planned to include in its agency review. They were D'Arcy Masius Benton and Bowles, Saatchi & Saatchi Advertising and, yes, J. Walter Thompson. In May 1989, the decision was made: Burger King split its agency account between Saatchi & Saatchi and D'Arcy Masius Benton and Bowles.

Chapter **9**

THE COLA WARS

T he marketing battle between Pepsi and Coca-Cola is certainly one of the greatest case studies in advertising and
marketing history. Many lessons are to be learned from
Pepsi's increased market share and Coke's reaction to it. Pepsi's use of positioning against the leader, and its reliance on
the same advertising theme for well over twenty years, served
it well. Coca-Cola's reaction to Pepsi's advertising and marketing, and its decision to change the formula of Coca-Cola, were
seen by many marketing experts to be one of the most serious
marketing blunders of all time. Less than eighty-seven days
after Coke introduced the new formula, the public outcry was
so vociferous that Coke brought back the original formula
under a new name, Coca-Cola Classic.™ The public's desire for
the original formula "flat caught us by surprise," admitted
Coke president Donald Keough. That is an amazing admis-
sion, coming as it does from what is certainly one of the country's foremost marketers. The simple fact of the matter is that
Coke misread the research, and in fact did not ask the right
questions, which led to the decision to scrap the original
brand.

The so-called Cola Wars between these two companies have a long and fascinating history. For many years, Coke absolutely dominated the market, so much so that Coke declined an opportunity to buy out Pepsi in 1933. Coke, led by Robert Woodruff, was far and away the leader when it came to cola, setting records for consumption not only in the United States but all over the world.

The skirmish between the two companies began to heat up during the 1960s. The last advertising campaign for Pepsi before BBDO was awarded the account in 1963 was called "The Sociables," which showed a variety of society figures drinking Pepsi. With the guidance of Pepsi's senior vice-president of creative services, Alan Pottasch, BBDO decided to do something that was unheard of at the time: focus on the user, or consumer, instead of the product. It is a technique now known as life-style advertising, the soft-focus selling of "warm fuzzies," as those in the trade say. The campaign was called the "Pepsi Generation."

One of the first efforts in the campaign used the tagline "Come Alive—You're in the Pepsi Generation." (The "in" was later deleted.) In the "Age of Aquarius," the phrase was perfect for the new generation making itself known at the time. In 1965 Pepsi strayed from the idea a bit with the introduction of another slogan: "Taste that Beats the Others Cold—Pepsi Pours It On." Research showed that consumers still remembered the "Pepsi Generation" theme the best, so the company revived it, with a slight difference: "You've Got a Lot to Live, and Pepsi's Got a Lot to Give. You're the Pepsi Generation." In 1975, the theme was still the Pepsi Generation, but with yet another twist: "Join the Pepsi People, Feelin' Free." All these variations on the same idea paid off. In 1974, for the first time ever, Pepsi pulled even with Coke in food-store sales, which would have been unthinkable even a decade earlier.

Then came the campaign that changed everything. Although it was planned by Pepsi purely as a promotion, it was eventually shown in markets all over the country and clearly scared Coca-Cola out of its wits. In fact, it was one of the things that eventually led Coke to tinker with its "Merchandise 7X," as Coke's secret formula was known.

The campaign was called "The Pepsi Challenge" and was dreamed up in 1975 by Larry Smith, who was in charge of Pepsi franchises in Texas. The South and the Southwest were the traditional power bases for the Atlanta-based Coke. In fact, Pepsi was getting whipped in Texas, holding on to only a tiny market share. Still, Smith felt that Pepsi was clearly the superior product: It had pulled even in food stores, where consumers have a choice, but because of Coke's sales in huge fast-food chains like McDonald's and Burger King, where Coke was the only soft drink sold, people were convinced that Coke was superior.

Smith worked with the in-house agency of the Southland Corporation's 7-Eleven convenience stores in a joint promotion to create "The Pepsi Challenge." The test, filmed behind a one-way mirror, was deceptively simple: Consumers were given two unmarked colas and were asked which one they liked best. Most of the people chose Pepsi, at a rate of 52 to 48, which gave Pepsi the right to say that it was the best-tasting soft drink.

The campaign began running in May 1975, and it quickly caught the attention of Coke, which responded with allegations of "misleading advertising." But the biggest shock for Coke came when it conducted its own taste tests. Coke found that its competitor's taste tests weren't false at all: Coke got similar results, a devasting blow, to say the least. To make matters worse, in that "pure" testing ground of supermarkets and food stores, Pepsi was starting to pull ahead of Coke.

Coke's public comments about the Pepsi Challenge included statements to the effect that Pepsi's choice of letters to identify blindly the two soft drinks had been biased. Unknown to Coke, Pepsi had used a variety of letters to identifiy the drinks; it countered Coke's move with a spot saying this the very next day. Coke also said that a small sip of either drink was not a fair way to judge: Coke would win if people got a long drink during which consumers could taste Coke's "zip." The market share for Pepsi immediately started to increase, and Pepsi extended the commercials to Houston.

Coke then decided to counter with its own taste tests, using loyal drinkers of Coke who would be certain to pick Coke over

> "Established brands have become like pillars. That's what Coca-Cola learned when it tried to remove one of the great pillars of all time."
>
> —Dr. Eugene Secunda, marketing professor
> Baruch College, New York City

Pepsi. But Coke achieved only a four-point win, numbers they didn't want to get back to Pepsi. Next Coke decided to have a taste test in which Coke and Pepsi were clearly identified. In that test, Coke was the preferred choice by a six-to-one margin.

From Houston, Pepsi expanded the test to Los Angeles, where Coke and Pepsi had almost an even market share. Research there showed that residents perceived that Coke was better than Pepsi—just the kind of market that Pepsi seemed to do best in with the "Challenge." Pepsi won in Los Angeles, feeding the juggernaut.

Although sales of both Coke and Pepsi were holding steady, the Challenge did something that clever positioning always accomplishes: In this case, it put the leader, Coke, on the defensive. This was the way the rest of the Cola Wars were played out—with Coke clearly on the defensive, and Pepsi on the attack.

In the late 1970s, Coke tried another tack—a series of commercials that used the popular actor Bill Cosby. Cosby made the point that if you are anything but number one, "you know what you want to be." He then held up a can of Coke. However, Cosby's popularity (which was widespread even before the success of his prime-time TV show) did not appear to blunt Pepsi's momentum. By 1983, the Pepsi Challenge was airing in almost 90 percent of U.S. markets.

The Challenge did much to injure Coke's pride, and for the first time the company was faced with a decision. Consumers clearly preferred the taste of Pepsi. If Coke did nothing, it was faced with the clear chance that Pepsi would eventually overtake Coke in more than just food-store sales. Coke's contracts with the huge fast-food chains such as McDonald's and Burger

King depended on its staying the number-one soft drink. Coke responded by having its research-and-development arm create several soft drinks that tasted sweeter, like Pepsi. In 1979, Coke's director of marketing research, Roy Stout, was charged with testing some of the new colas. The information he gathered would determine just where Coke decided to strike next.

In the meantime, Coke and Pepsi's attention was diverted for a while by another product, Coke's new diet drink called Diet Coke.™ This is what is known in the advertising and marketing business as a **line extension**. Line extensions can be risky undertakings. When you create a new product, particularly one that uses part of the name of another brand (Coke), you run the risk of **cannibalizing**, or cutting into the sales of, the original product. Also, Coke had another diet drink on the market called Tab.™

Diet Coke turned out to be a gold mine. It was introduced in August 1982 with a huge press conference and one of the most expensive commercials the company had ever made, an extravaganza costing $1.5 million and starring a multitude of Hollywood stars, as well as the Rockettes from Radio City Music Hall. And, although some Tab drinkers switched to Diet Coke, the two diet drinks tasted sufficiently different to create two different niches in the marketplace. By 1983, Diet Coke was the best-selling diet drink in the United States, and by 1984 it had overtaken 7 Up™ as the number-three soft drink in the country. This was an incredible coup for Coke—the Diet Coke launch clearly qualified as the most successful new product launch in soft-drink history. Much of the credit for this bold move was given to Roberto Goizueta, who had replaced Robert Woodruff as chairman.

About the time of the Diet Coke success, Pepsi had installed a new president—Roger Enrico, an astute marketing mind who was determined to win the Cola Wars. Enrico had a very clear idea of what he wanted Pepsi to be. He decided to get away from the Pepsi Challenge and refocus the company's efforts on the Pepsi Generation. BBDO and its creative chief, Phil Dusenberry, created eye-catching new spots for Pepsi. One showed a spaceship hovering over both a Coke and Pepsi vending machine, then "beaming up" the Pepsi machine. As Enrico later said, "It doesn't say a word about Pepsi tasting better and it's the best damn Pepsi Challenge commercial ever dreamed up."

About the same time, Enrico was approached by promoter Don King, who asked whether Pepsi would be interested in sponsoring the world tour for the singing group the Jacksons. This was right on the heels of the phenomenal success of Michael Jackson's album *Thriller,* the top-selling album of all time. Jackson had also made an electric appearance on a Motown special doing the famous "moonwalk" dance. He was very hot, and Pepsi wanted him. The asking price was considered astronomical—$5 million.

Enrico bit, hoping that his superiors would see the genius of hooking up with the country's most popular entertainer, a shining example of the Pepsi Generation. Never mind that Jackson did not drink Pepsi (or any other soft drink, for that matter), nor would he in the TV commercial. Pepsi was delighted to get him. The $5 million asking price—the most money anyone has ever been paid to appear in a television commercial—included two commercials with Michael and his siblings, sponsorship of the Victory Tour (which included Pepsi's name on the signage in the stadiums, on the tickets, etc.) and personal appearances at press conferences.

The signing of Jackson was hot news. Bob Giraldi, who directed Jackson in the sizzling video for the song "Beat It," was then signed to direct the TV spots. At a press conference held to announce the signing, shy Michael Jackson told Enrico just what he wanted to hear: "Roger, I'm going to make Coke wish they were Pepsi."

The ads were to make its premiere on the Grammy Awards broadcast, only a few months away, meaning that there was little time to get every element perfect. In the meantime, a deal was struck, with MTV, which agreed to run the spots for free if they were given an exclusive the night before the Grammys. Pepsi agreed.

About this time some problems cropped up with the filming of the commercial. Michael Jackson, a highly creative entertainer, did not like the music or the storyboards that were presented to him. He had also decided that he did not want to be overexposed, and therefore did not want to be in either spot for more than four seconds. Needless to say, this did not go over well with Pepsi. The Jacksons did not show for the first shoot, which cost Pepsi $200,000. Soon lawyers were called in to settle the fray. Michael Jackson, whom Pepsi almost always heard from third-hand through either Don King, his lawyers or parents, finally reigned: Since he didn't like the music selected, he offered Pepsi the use of "Billie Jean" for free. The Pepsi people were ecstatic, of course: The use of one of the hottest songs in the country could easily have cost in the millions.

Phil Dusenberry and the BBDO crew came up with two spots. One showed the family behind the scenes, drinking Pepsi (except for Michael), just prior to a concert. There were fireworks, and then the Jacksons came onto the stage, performing the new improved version of "Billie Jean," with Pepsi lyrics ("You're the Pepsi Generation"). The other spot was more lyrical. It showed Alfonso Ribeiro, a young dancer from the Broadway show *The Tap Dance Kid,* perfectly mimicking all of Michael Jackson's dancing moves. As he moonwalks, he backs up into Michael Jackson and his brothers—and is surprised and elated at whom he's had the good fortune to meet.

Then came any advertising executive's worst nightmare. During filming, the pyrotechnics used during the fireworks segment of the concert spot sent Michael Jackson's hair up in flames. Jackson was rushed to a burn center, and the event made the evening news. Pepsi was terrified that Jackson's many fans would never pick up a can of Pepsi again. There was also talk of Jackson's suing. Then there was haggling over the look of the spots; Jackson was not pleased with them. They showed his face too often, he said, and he had to take off his sunglasses, which he did not want to do.

Finally, with the commercials edited and re-edited to get just the "right" amount of Michael, they were ready to be shown on the Grammys. Meanwhile, a huge publicity apparatus created so much advance word about the commercial that consumers and the press the world over were clamoring for a glimpse of the spots. As it turned out, Jackson cleaned up at the Grammys, winning a record-breaking eight awards. Most important for Pepsi, 83 million people saw him spin and strut in the commercials.

In 1984, Coke was beginning to realize its worst fears: If it didn't do something, it was in real danger of being overtaken by Pepsi in market share. It was a truly horrifying proposition: Coke was outspending Pepsi by $100 million in advertising and promotion, and still its market share was dwindling. Coke had to figure out what was wrong. It was outspending Pepsi in advertising, but was its advertising as good? Coke figured that it had always had its share of memorable ads, too. There was "The Real Thing," "Have a Coke and a Smile" and, one of its big winners, a spot featuring the football player "Mean Joe" Green offering his Coke to a young fan. Even the "I'd Like to Teach the World to Sing" spot was still trotted out on occasion around the winter holidays. No, Coke's advertising worked.

That meant that there was little choice but to focus on the Coca-Cola taste, the secret Merchandise 7X. In 1983, Coke formed a team, eventually known as Project Kansas, to explore the possibility of a reformulation. The project proceeded with the utmost secrecy: All paperwork was shredded, and anyone from the company or advertising agency who leaked information would be fired if caught.

First the research department was charged with finding out how willing the public would be to accept a new Coke. This was challenging, because the company had to do the research without tipping its hand to the public or the press. More than 2,000 consumers were shown a storyboard saying that Coke had added a new ingredient to make it sweeter, and then Coke asked the consumers questions about the proposed change. The research showed that from 10 to 12 percent of Coke drinkers would be upset, but that half of those would get over it. In addition, a number of loyal Pepsi drinkers indicated they would be interested in a new formulation of Coca-Cola.

Focus groups were also used during this initial period, and Coke learned some very confusing things about people's perceptions of the soft drink. For one thing, people almost always said that they liked Coke best, even though they might actually buy a number of other soft drinks. This showed that what people said and what they actually did were two very different things. The groups also indicated that tampering with Coke was a kind of blasphemy that should not be tolerated.

So, although Coke saw that there would be some resistance to the idea of change, Coke proceeded with its plan to formulate a better soft drink. Whatever objections were voiced, Coke was sure, would be silenced by a superior-tasting drink.

Coke executives wanted to make a decision as soon as possible. The company's centennial celebration was planned for 1986; it was a huge event that took over the city of Atlanta for a week and to which Coke executives and bottlers from all over the world were invited. Coke executives didn't want a new product to take away any interest from the centennial hoopla, so they wanted either to press forward with a new brand immediately or hold off until after the celebration.

In late 1984, four Coke executives met and decided to go ahead with the new "improved" taste of Coke. The first step was to talk to Coke's advertising agency, McCann-Erickson, about how to position the brand, what to call it and what kind of advertising to run. The McCann executives were shocked, to say the least. There had been some talk that Coke would introduce another brand, but no clue that Coke would tinker with the original formulation.

Positioning was considered crucial: Coke did not want to admit that Pepsi had tested higher in the taste tests over the years, yet it would be obvious to anyone that there was some very good reason that Coke would change a brand that had done it so proud for so many years and was one of the most recognizable brands in the world.

McCann executives began working on the project around the clock amid great secrecy. The Coke research team, meanwhile, was on the road, testing two formulations of Coke: one as sweet as Pepsi, the other a little sweeter. Both drinks scored higher than Pepsi, so a decision was made to go with the sweeter drink. Ironically, Coke's ads at the time hawked the drink as better than Pepsi because it was less sweet.

During this time it was decided that the word *new* could never be associated with the new formulation, because it implied too drastic a change to the consumer. A number of advertising themes were tossed around for the new formulation, among them "It's All Right Here" and "We've Got a Taste for You." The current Coke tagline was "Coke Is It."

On April 19, 1985, news media across the country were sent a press release saying that on the following Tuesday the company would hold a press conference "at which time the most significant soft-drink marketing development in the country's nearly 100-year history will be announced."

The timing of the release was intended to give the press plenty of time to guess what the big news was—and run stories about it. But the announcement also allowed Pepsi to outflank Coke, and get in the first word before Coke said anything. Although Pepsi executives knew that Coke had been working on a new formulation, they thought it would be a line extension rather than a new formulation. After the initial shock, they decided that Pepsi would take the offensive and declare that they had won the Cola Wars over Coke.

Pepsi decided to run an ad to this effect, but was undecided about what it should say. Finally, it was decided to reprint the memo that Roger Enrico had written to Pepsi employees about Coke's move:

"It gives me great pleasure to offer each of you my heartiest congratulations. After eighty-seven years of going at it eyeball to eyeball, the other guy just blinked! . . . Maybe they realized what most of us have know for years: Pepsi Tastes Better Than Coke."

Pepsi also decided to give its employees a day off to celebrate and to demonstrate that Pepsi was confident and sure it was the main reason Coke was changing the formula.

Coke held its press conference at Lincoln Center in New York City, with satellite hook-up to cities all around the United States. Roberto Goizueta called Coke's decision to reformulate "the surest move ever made because the new taste of Coke was shaped by the taste of the consumer."

The reporters on hand had hundreds of questions, not the least of which was: "To what extent are you introducing this product to meet the Pepsi Challenge?" Coke denied it, of course, but it was a question that was to dog the new Coke for months.

Coke had to be aware that the penetrating questions about how much the new drink tasted like Pepsi would come up. Indeed, Pepsi was busy telling reporters how Pepsi had been steadily taking market share away from Coke and how Pepsi had always outperformed Coke in taste tests. Pepsi also staged its own press conference just down the street, giving consumers free samples and declaring itself the winner of the Cola Wars.

The negative response—mainly the outcry from consumers that Coke had taken away an old favorite—poured in almost immediately after the announcement. More than 1,000 phone calls a day were pouring into Coke's headquarters, and press coverage was almost universally negative—mostly in the vein that Pepsi was beating Coke, and that Coke had ruined an American tradition by changing its formula. Coke wasn't surprised, since it had expected a number of consumers to be unhappy.

Coke saturated the airwaves with spots showing Bill Cosby promoting Coke's new taste. Pepsi responded with two spots: One showed a teen-aged girl writing a letter to Pepsi asking the company why Coke had decided to create a new formula, then taking a big sip of Pepsi and announcing to the camera, "Now I know why."

In another spot, called "Wilbur," Pepsi showed three elderly men chatting while sitting on a park bench. One of them lamented that he stuck with Coke through many years, and that there must be a big reason why they were changing the formula. "Right big," said his friend, nodding and taking a big sip of Pepsi.

In Coke's hometown of Atlanta, consumers were given the old and new versions in a taste test—and the original formula won. The test was especially embarrassing for Coke because two of the tasters were the owner of one of the city's biggest fast-food chains and the local historian, both of whom had been on the dais as supporters when Coke made the original announcement.

News stories all over the United States told of long-time Coke drinkers who were so loyal that they drove hundreds of miles to bottlers of Coke so that they could stockpile the original version. A Seattle man protested by starting a group called the Old Cola Drinkers of America.

By June it became obvious to Coke that something had gone badly wrong. Even though taste tests done by Coke after the press conference still showed that consumers liked the new Coke better than Pepsi, the decision to change the drink touched a nerve that ran much deeper than anything having to do with taste. Consumers felt a strong tie to Coke. Those earlier comments about changing the original formula being tantamount to blasphemy now sounded ringingly accurate.

Just eighty-seven days after Coke brought out its new version, the company swallowed its pride and held another news conference announcing that it would bring back the original formula, to be called Coca-Cola Classic, and continue to sell the new formula under the flagship Coca-Cola name.

The letters that the Coke executives read at this second press conference showed how deeply feeling ran about the new drink. "Dear Chief Dodo," began one.

CEO Donald Keough owned up to Coke's mistake, saying it was a story "which will please every humanist and will probably have Harvard professors puzzling for years. The simple fact is that all the time and money and skill poured into consumer research on the new Coca-Cola could not measure or reveal the deep and abiding emotional attachment to original Coke. . . . Passion was something wonderful that caught us by surprise. It is a wonderful American mystery and you cannot measure it any more than you can measure love, pride or patriotism."

ABC News interrupted the TV show "General Hospital" to make the announcement. Consumers were thrilled: More than 12,000 approving phone calls came into the company headquarters. Not long afterward, Coke Classic began to outsell the new formulation by a wide margin.

After the new Coke-old Coke fiasco, Coke began referring to its advertising and marketing efforts as being part of something it called megabranding. The idea, Coke said, was to promote all of its Coke products—Cherry Coke,™ Diet Coke and the Classic and new formulas—under one umbrella. Was that a smart move? If Coke was hoping to say that it had the most sales of product by lumping them all in one basket, it was a stroke of genius. But many detractors—Pepsi being the main one—said the idea was to draw attention away from the fact that Pepsi now had the number-one brand if only a single product was counted.

Are the Cola Wars over? Hardly. The two companies still go at each other as the top marketers in the country, each having learned a lot from this latest, and biggest, skirmish in the Cola Wars.

Chapter 10

MARLBORO: SELLING THE AMERICAN COWBOY

I n 1955, the American habit of smoking cigarettes had never been stronger. According to government statistics, the country lit up 382 billion cigarettes that year, 2,262 for every American. Among the less-successful contenders for that huge market was an obscure brand for women called Marlboro.

Since then, the image of smoking has veered from glamorous to deadly, and Americans now smoke fewer and fewer cigarettes each year. But more and more of the cigarettes smoked—now one in every four—are Marlboros. Backed by the longest-running ad campaign for any major product, Marlboros alone bring in sales of more than $8 billion a year. That makes Marlboro, not Coca-Cola or Tide™ or Crest™ the best-selling packaged-good brand in the world.

To pull off that marketing feat in an eroding market, Philip Morris Co., Inc. has nurtured Marlboro with deft marketing and had the good sense to stick with one of the world's most enduring commercial images—the American cowboy. Marlboro has grown share point by share point for more than thirty years. Over that time, Philip Morris and its advertising agency, Leo Burnett, have groomed its cowboy for the international market and sent it out to nearly every country in the free world. The company continually mines the vast equity built up in the Marlboro name to produce line extensions, such as Marlboro Lights, that burn up share in every segment of the cigarette market.

As a result, Marlboro is also the world's most powerful brand. Marlboro's advertising consistently scores among America's best-liked print campaigns—a remarkable feat for a product most people disapprove of, and a testament to the sheer power of the brand itself.

As the world's best-selling cigarette, Marlboro sits atop a pedestal that is crumbling beneath it. Government statistics show that the percentage of American adults who smoke drops slightly each year and now stands at 27 percent, or 47 million people. That's down from 40 percent in 1964, the year the U.S. Surgeon General first warned of a link between smoking and cancer, heart disease and other health problems. In a recent poll, 55 percent of adults favored a complete ban on smoking in all public places, and, astonishingly, 25 percent of smokers agreed.

Philip Morris could preserve the Marlboro brand by extending it into other businesses—putting the Marlboro name on non-cigarette products—a strategy Philip Morris executives don't dismiss. And if the odds are against it, consider Marlboro's history of beating the odds all along. First launched as a women's brand in 1924, Marlboro came in a white box with script lettering and the slogan "Mild as May." Women smokers didn't buy the taste claim, so Philip Morris, desperate for a way to differentiate the brand, added an ivory-colored tip. No dice. Women complained that this showed lipstick stains. Philip Morris made the tip red. That, too, proved a resounding failure. Philip Morris withdrew the brand in the late 1940s.

Marlboro returned in the mid-1950s after American Tobacco made Pall Mall™ the first cigarette with a filter tip. Figuring it should have a filter cigarette, too, Philip Morris filter-tipped Marlboros, and this time pitched the brand to men.

The big breakthrough came when Joe Cullman, then chief executive of Philip Morris, and Leo Burnett invented the new image for Marlboro—the cowboy. Shortly after Philip Morris relaunched the brand, Leo Burnett unveiled ads featuring the notorious cowpoke and the tagline "The news has come out of the West."

The news was that Marlboro was the first cigarette to come in a flip-top box, and the brand started showing signs of life. The 8.5 percent share Marlboro held in 1955 would make it a successful brand today, but an 8.5 percent share in 1955 made Marlboro an also-ran. Still, it was a start. As smokers switched from non-filters like Camel™ to filters, many chose Marlboro, helping the cowboy from Marlboro country ride to a share of 13 percent by 1968. That made Marlboro the number-two brand, behind R. J. Reynolds Tobacco Co.'s Winston™ brand, which had a 20 percent share.

Marlboro might have spent years chasing Winston were it not for an event that looked like a catastrophe for all cigarette marketers at the time. In 1970, the tobacco companies, seeing that popular sentiment was mounting for a ban, voluntarily withdrew their advertising from television. Anti-smoking advocates were getting equal time for their very effective messages, in effect canceling out costly cigarette television advertising. Since Marlboro advertising ran almost entirely on television, the brand looked particularly vulnerable.

Instead, the pull-out from broadcast advertising proved an immense benefit. Most cigarette marketers retooled for the new era of print. As a result, their advertising often started from scratch in the new environment. Philip Morris, however, decided to stick with the cowboy for its Marlboro print ads. The image not only transferred exceptionally well, but it also gave Marlboro continuity at a time when its competitors lost much of their momentum. In 1975, Marlboro overtook Winston as the number-one brand, and it has reigned unchallenged since then.

The basic positioning has changed very little over the years. The Leo Burnett agency, which still handles Marlboro and devotes about twenty-five staffers to the account, has never used professional models as Marlboro Men. Burnett talent scouts are constantly scouring cowboy country for ranch hands with Marlboro Man potential. These ranch hands, and a number of other "real-men" types, form a revolving pool of Marlboro cowboys. And while the Marlboro marketing group does conduct focus groups and one-on-one interviews with smokers, the campaign owes little to formal research. The company itself has fifteen marketers assigned to Marlboro in the United States, and another fifty executives working on Marlboro's international business, mostly adapting the Marlboro country theme to local advertising and promotions.

Reaching smokers gets trickier all the time. The shrinking market makes mass advertising less and less efficient. RJR and the other cigarette marketers have cut back on advertising and shifted marketing dollars into promotion. Philip Morris promotes heavily—country music events and sports events, including the Virginia Slims tennis sponsorships, are Philip Morris's venues of choice, having spent an estimated $85 million on sports sponsorship in 1988, compared to $58 million for RJR. But it has kept ad spending relatively constant on Marlboro, partly because the campaign has been so effective. The result is that Marlboro's "share of voice" in cigarette advertising is rising.

Theoretically, Marlboro's dependence on advertising leaves it vulnerable to industry critics seeking to muzzle tobacco marketers. Anti-smoking forces are pushing for a ban on cigarette advertising; several bills introduced in Congress also strike at tobacco advertising, either by seeking to restrict it outright or to limit the tax deductibility of advertising expenditures. Still, this remains a mostly domestic problem. The Marlboro Man is still riding high around the globe.

Chapter 11

SO, YOU WANT TO BE IN ADVERTISING?

Well, be forewarned, so do a lot of other people. Advertising tends to be one of those businesses, like modeling and acting, that attracts legions of hopefuls. Still, if you are talented and very persistent, there is a good chance that you can land a job in the field.

Advertising is a realm in which a college degree or even an education in advertising doesn't necessarily guarantee an entry. While account executives might find a business degree helpful, and media buyers certainly need a proficiency with numbers, a creative person can literally come from any background, and, usually, the more colorful the better.

It's not uncommon, for example, to find advertising people with backgrounds in psychiatric medicine or stand-up comedy—sometimes in the same person! Louise McNamee, who became the first woman to have her name added to a big established agency (Della Femina Travisano & Partners, now Della Femina, McNamee WCRS), was a social worker and kindergarten teacher before working her way up the ranks in the

> "Advertising is the most fun you can have with your clothes on."
>
> —Jerry Della Femina, in *From Those Wonderful Folks Who Gave You Pearl Harbor*

agency business. Experience with people, and with different kinds of living, only enhances an agency person's understanding of the world and his or her ability to communicate with it.

Is it worth getting an advertising degree at a college, or going to a special school to build up a creative portfolio? It certainly can't hurt. Learning the basic lingo of how agencies work, and why different campaigns succeed or fail, can only enhance your chances of being hired. A number of schools have opened that specialize in the creative areas of copywriting, art direction and design where students learn all the basics, from product design to television production. Most important, they are constantly called on to produce ideas and actual ads, the idea being to simulate the work and environment of a real agency.

Still, there is no guarantee that a degree will get you a job. It might help you get a foot in the door, but the rest is up to you. As more and more agencies are consolidated, the number of advertising jobs becomes fewer and the competition more intense. As with almost any field, getting what you want takes persistence and drive.

The good news is that advertising is one of those businesses in which you can work yourself to the top. Thus, starting out as an assistant, secretary or intern is not a bad idea. The advertising agency business is full of people who are now agency presidents who started in the mailroom, or creative people who started out as secretaries. If you have any talent at all, there is a good chance that the agency will notice you and want to use you in a higher capacity. Before you know it, you could climb aboard the fast track. Also, as we've seen, advertising agencies aren't the only places where there are jobs having to do with advertising.

Times are tight, as far as budgets go, so fewer agencies have training programs. These were once the bread and butter of many shops, a way to discover and nurture new talent in an agency's own image. Still, some of the biggest agencies continue to have them.

If you are a creative person, there is also the possibility of free-lancing—that is, working directly for a client or agency on certain projects. Free-lancers fill primarily creative roles—as copywriters, illustrators and art directors—and usually have a little experience under their belt at an agency. As the agency business gets more and more fragmented, there are even free-lance media people, called in only for special projects.

What are the drawbacks of working in advertising?

It is a mercurial business.

With clients firing agencies, and companies being eaten up by mergers, there is simply no job security, no matter how far up the ladder you are. If a huge piece of business like IBM walks out the door, as it did for two large New York agencies in 1989, many people are usually fired—in this case, ninety at one agency.

Pressure from the "it was due yesterday" syndrome.

For agencies working with retailers, which often have to place new ads literally every day, there is the constant headache of deadlines.

Bad tempers and huge egos.

Advertising attracts some of the most talented people, but with that talent there often come, shall we say, difficult personalities. That means walking on eggshells at times, or huge fights at others. One Atlanta agency account executive was startled one day when he walked into a presentation only to find the two partners wrestling in the midst of an argument on the floor—with the client trying to separate them!

But there are plenty of great things about advertising. The work is usually interesting, and the people certainly are. Some advertising jobs boast opportunities for travel, and most offer lots of entertainment. Media buyers at most agencies are regularly taken out to lunch by magazine reps who want them to

> "Advertising is the only business in the world where you are rewarded for masochistic tendencies."

buy space in their books. Other perks include tickets to sporting events and the theater, holiday gifts and the like. This is a double-edged sword; some agencies don't allow perks so that people are not at all beholden to or even influenced by them. On a more serious level, being part of a team that produces effective, even artful advertising can be a truly thrilling experience.

Advertising is also a business in which the top talents can earn an astronomical amount of money. A twenty-nine-year-old art director moved to New York City to work for a top agency at a salary of $100,000 a year. He left less than six months later, a little bored by the work, for a job in another city—where an agency had added $20,000 to the kitty. It's not unusual for agency CEO's to earn as much as $500,000 a year, when profit-sharing and perks are thrown in.

In *Adweek* magazine's annual salary survey, average salaries for 1988 were as follows:

- chairman/CEO: $106,000.
- agency copywriter: $46,000
- account executive: $41,000
- art director: $36,000
- media buyer or planner: $26,000

Keep in mind that these represent national averages, so the salaries in big cities like New York, Chicago and Los Angeles were somewhat higher.

To keep up with what is happening in the advertising world, read the advertising columns in *The New York Times* and *The Wall Street Journal,* and trade magazines like *Adweek* and *Advertising Age*. With a little luck and a lot of persistence, that elusive agency job will be yours.

GLOSSARY

account executive: the employee of an ad agency who coordinates plans with the client

added value: a quality (often intangible) that distinguishes one product from another

advertorial: a section of a magazine designed to look like editorial pages that is actually paid for and designed by an advertiser

art director: the creative at an ad agency who designs an ad

brand: any trademarked name assigned to a specific product or service

brand loyalty: consumer allegiance to a particualr brand

broadcast: any programming transmitted over the airwaves via one of the "Big Three" networks (ABC, NBC and CBS)

cablecast: transmission of cable programming (broadcast refers to programming transmitted over the airwaves)

cannibalization: occurs when one brand cuts into sales of a brand marketed by the same company

commercial break: when broadcasts are interrupted to transmit advertising

comparative advertising: advertising that compares one product with another

consumer recall: the degree to which consumers remember ads for a product

copywriter: creative at an advertising agency who actually writes the copy for a print, radio or television ad

creative director: the employee of an ad agency responsible for overseeing the production of copy and visuals for ads

demographics: the statistical characteristics of human populations (such as age and income); used to identify markets

direct marketing: any marketing effort that appeals directly to the consumer

event marketing: associating a product with an event such as a rock concert or arts festival through sponsorship or other tie-in

focus groups: consumer panels that provide agencies with information about how they feel about a certain product or advertising campaign

generic: refers to a whole product class rather than a particular brand; also refers to cheaper "no-name" brands

image advertising: ads that rely on intangible rather than specific product attributes

independents: television stations that function independently of the networks

line extension: a new product brought out under an existing brand name

lowballing: the practice by which agencies charge less than the standard 15 percent commission in order to win an account

markets: the customers for a product or service

market research: the study of consumer likes and dislikes, performed so that companies can more specifically and knowledgeably "target" specific audiences of consumers with products and services

market share: the percentage of sales in a product category claimed by one product, brand or company

media budget: that portion of a marketing budget allocated to purchasing space in print media or time on broadcast or cable media

media buy: the purchase of space in print media or time in broadcast or cable media

media buyer: the person at an advertising agency who actually purchases media time

media planner: the person at an advertising agency who oversees the media budget

narrowcast: a type of programming that is viewed by a specific minority segment of the population

people meters: electronic push-button method of recording who is watching certain television shows

premium: bonus offered to consumers who buy a product

ratings: the percentage of the population watching or listening to a television or radio show at a specific time

reach: the number of people who view a particular show

research: examining competitive products, interviewing consumers, etc., in order to prepare the most effective advertising campaign

roll-out: the introduction of a new product into additional markets

spot: short term for an ad running on television or radio

spot media buy: small purchases of radio or television time on a local television or radio station

superstation: an independent station that is distributed via satellite to cable stations around the country; WTBS in Atlanta, WOR in New York and WGN in Chicago are examples

tagline: the advertising slogan or theme-line of an ad campaign

test market: the area in which a manufacturer sells a new product on a trial basis

umbrella campaign: ads covering more than one product marketed by one manufacturer

zapper: a television viewer who used a remote-control device to switch channels during commercials or fast-forward during re-plays of taped programs so as to avoid, or "zap," advertising

SUGGESTED READING

BOOKS

Adman: Morris Hite's Methods for Winning the Ad Game
Russ Pate. E-Hart Press, Dallas, TX, 1988

Advertising and the American Dream
Roland Marchand. University of California Press, Berkeley, CA, 1985

Advertising Career Directory
Ronald Fry. The Career Press Inc., Hawthorne, NJ, 1987

Advertising Manager's Handbook
Richard H. Stansfield, Dartnell Corporation, Chicago, IL, 1982

The Advertising Manual
Stephen Baker. John Wiley & Sons, New York, NY, 1988

Confessions of an Advertising Man
David Ogilvy. Crown Publishers, Inc., New York, NY, 1963

Fifty Rules to Keep a Client Happy
Fred Poppe. Harper & Row, New York, NY, 1987

From Those Wonderful Folks Who Brought You Pearl Harbor
Jerry Della Femina. Simon and Schuster, New York, NY, 1970

How to Save Your Clients from Themselves and Yourself from Them
Curtis Hills. Olde & Oppenheim Publishers, Phoenix, AZ, 1988

I Love Advertising
Whit Hobbs. Adweek Books, New York, NY, 1985

Ogilvy on Advertising
David Ogilvy. Crown Publishers, Inc., New York, NY, 1983

Power and Persuasion on Madison Avenue: The Image Makers
William Meyers. Times Books, New York, NY, 1984

Radio Advertising: The Authoritative Handbook
Bob Schulberg. NTC Business Books, Lincolnwood, IL, 1989

So You Want to Be in Advertising?
Ed Caffrey. Simon & Schuster, New York, NY, 1988

Television and Its Audience
Patrick Barwise and Andrew Ehrenberg. Sage Publications, London, 1988

The Trouble with Advertising: A View from the Inside
John O'Toole. Times Books, New York, NY, 1980

Which Ad Pulled Best? Fifty Case Histories on How to Write Ads That Work
Philip Ward Burton and Scott Purvis. NTC Business Books, Lincolnwood, IL, 1987

MAGAZINES

Advertising Age
Published weekly on Mondays by Crain Communications, Inc., 740 N. Rush Street, Chicago, IL 60611-2590

Adweek
Published weekly on Mondays by ASM Communications, Inc., 49 East 21st Street, New York, NY 10010

NEWSLETTERS

The Gallagher Report
"A confidential letter to management, marketing, and advertising executives."
Published weekly by The Gallagher Report, Inc., 230 Park Avenue, New York, NY 10017

INDEX

ABOUT THE AUTHOR

Susan Sewell is managing editor of *Adweek/East* in New York. A native of Atlanta, Georgia, she was previously the managing editor of *Adweek/Southeast* in Atlanta, and a reporter and editor for the *Marietta Daily Journal* and Neighbor newspapers. She is a graduate of Georgia State University.

If you're mystified by the buzz-word world of business insiders and MBAs, then **BUSINESS SMARTS**—offering straightforward, accessible, entertaining advice about the basics of business—is for you! Look for these handy guides from **Price Stern Sloan:**

ACCOUNTING MADE EASY

A critical aspect of any business, accounting is also one of the most intimidating. *Accounting Made Easy* shows how to decipher annual reports and balance sheets, explains how the accounting profession works and details the changing face of the industry today.

BUSINESS FINANCE MADE EASY

From merger mania and leveraged buyouts to the basics of reading the financial and business news, *Business Finance Made Easy* will help the reader gain confidence in an increasingly complex field.

MARKETING MADE EASY

Any product must have great marketing to be successful. *Marketing Made Easy* covers all the essentials: product placement and promotion, product life-cycle and positioning, how product and profit are tied to price variations and more.